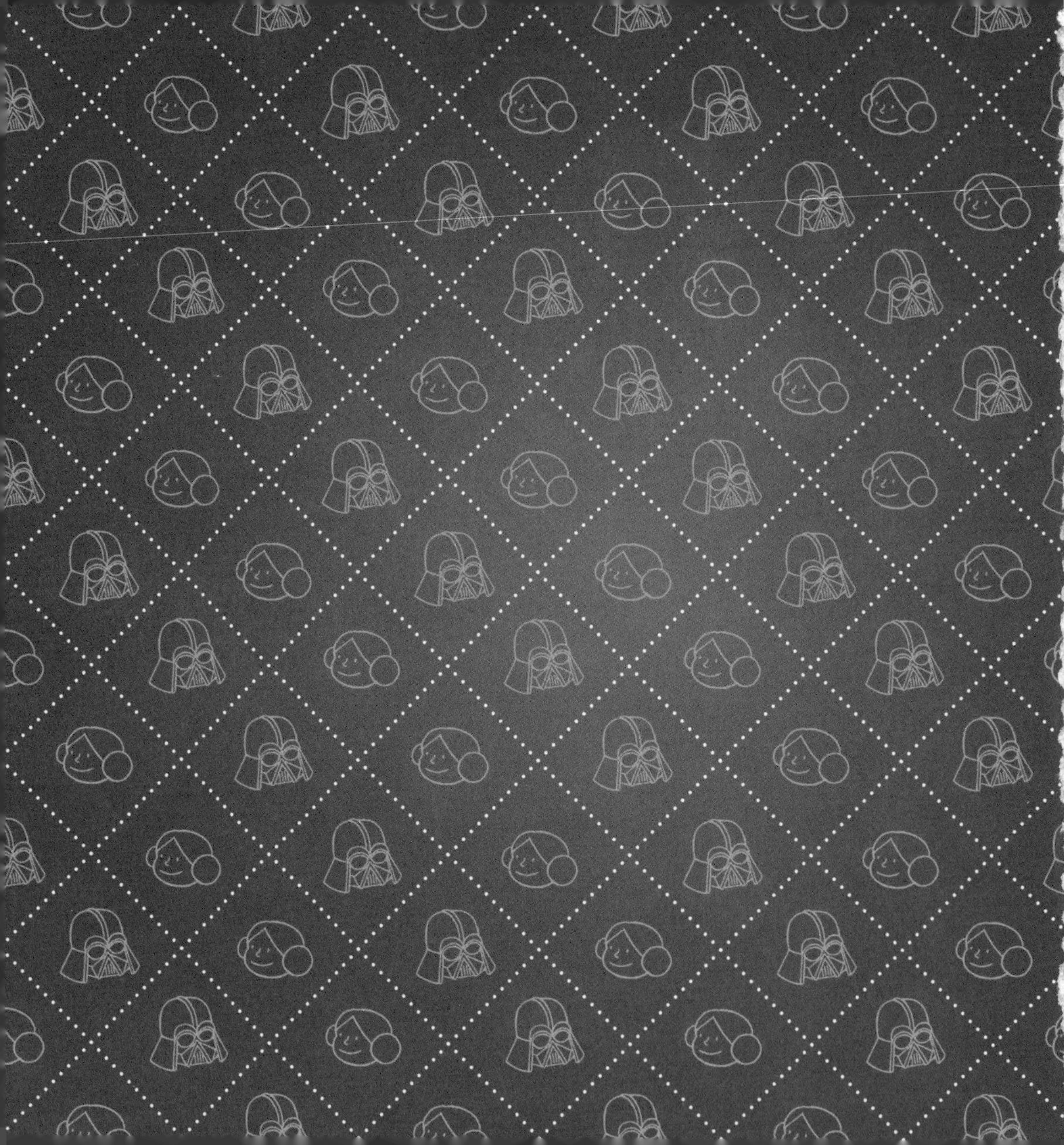

VADER'S™
little princess

JEFFREY BROWN

CHRONICLE BOOKS
SAN FRANCISCO

LIBRARY OF CONGRESS CATALOGING-IN-PUBLICATION DATA: AVAILABLE

ISBN 978-1-4521-1869-7

MANUFACTURED IN CANADA.
WRITTEN AND DRAWN BY JEFFREY BROWN
DESIGNED BY MICHAEL MORRIS

THANKS TO STEVE MOCKUS, J.W. RINZLER, MARC GERALD, MICHAEL
MORRIS, AND MY FAMILY. SPECIAL THANKS TO RYAN GERMICK
AND MICHEAL LOPEZ AT GOOGLE FOR THE ORIGINAL INSPIRATION
TO MAKE DARTH VADER AND SON. MOST OF ALL, THANKS TO
GEORGE LUCAS FOR MAKING GREAT TOYS AND LETTING ME PLAY
WITH THEM.

10 9 8 7 6 5

CHRONICLE BOOKS LLC
680 SECOND STREET
SAN FRANCISCO, CA 94107
WWW. CHRONICLEBOOKS. COM

WWW. STARWARS. COM

A long time ago in a galaxy far,
far away....

Episode Three and Three-Quarters:
VADER'S LITTLE PRINCESS

Darth Vader, Dark Lord
of the Sith, continues to
rule the Galactic Empire and
is out to destroy the heroic
Rebel Alliance. Meanwhile,
he must raise his young
daughter, Leia, as she grows
from a sweet little girl -
into a rebellious teenager....

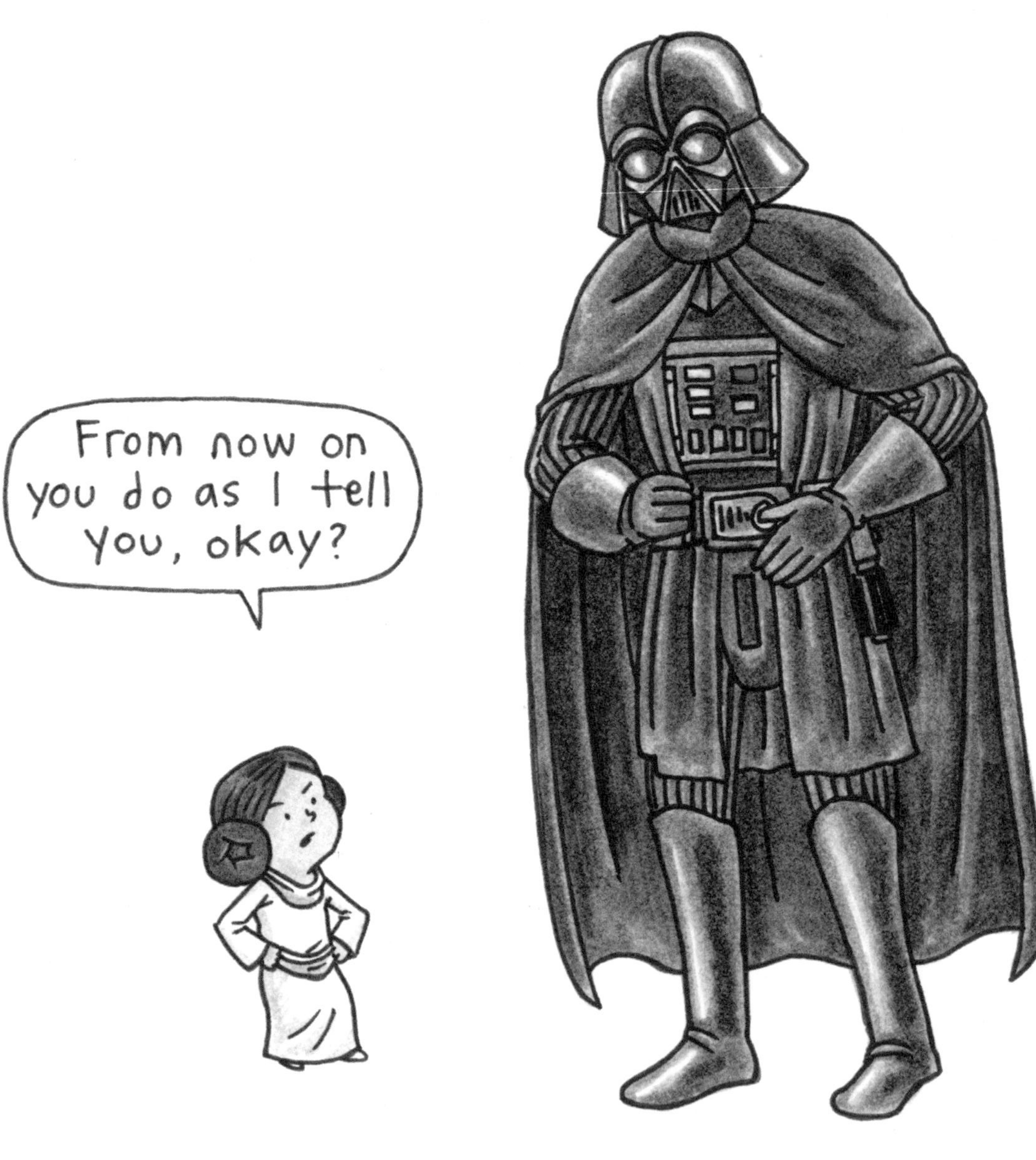
From now on you do as I tell you, okay?

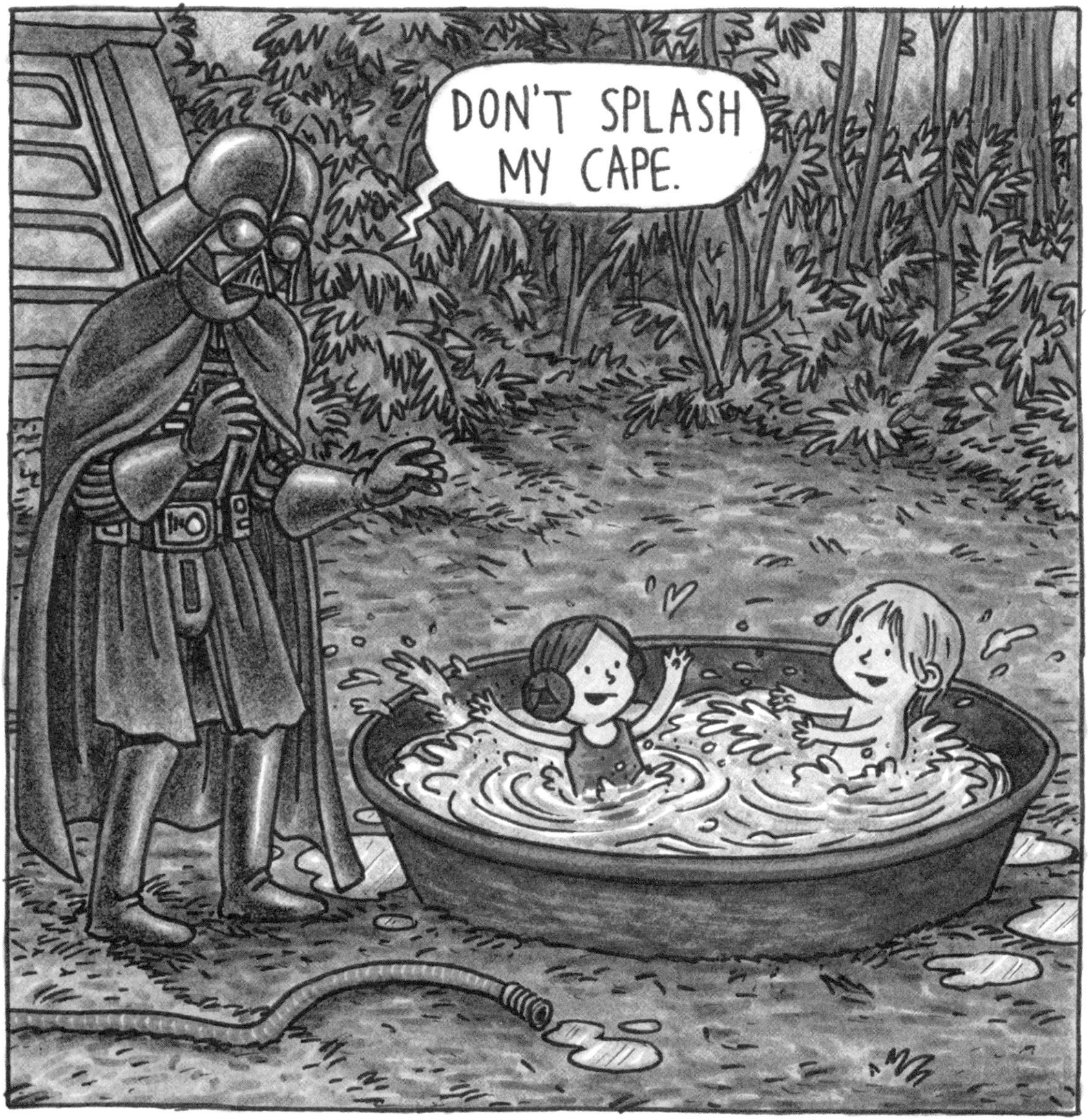
DON'T SPLASH MY CAPE.

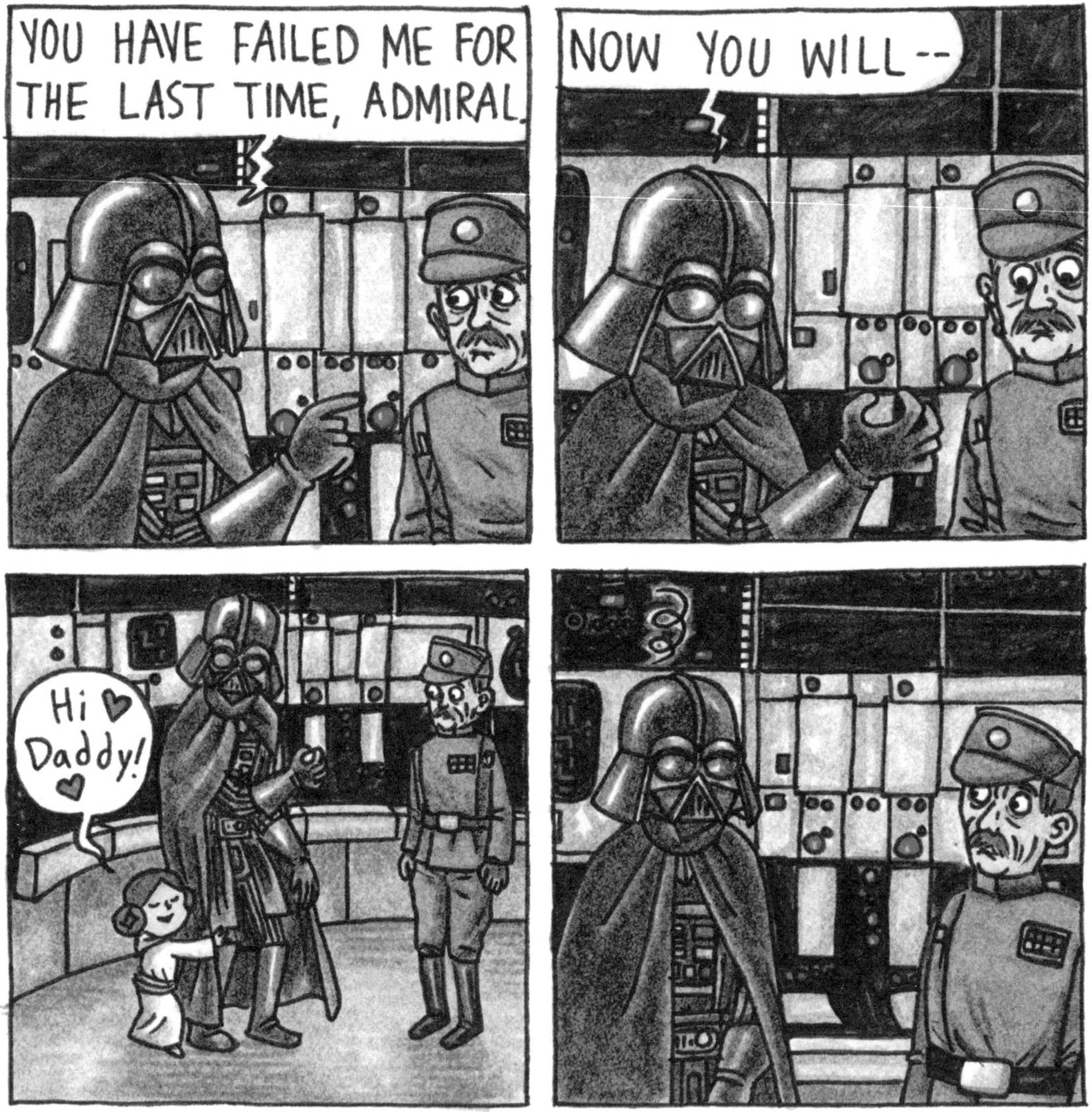
YOU HAVE FAILED ME FOR THE LAST TIME, ADMIRAL.
NOW YOU WILL--
Hi Daddy!

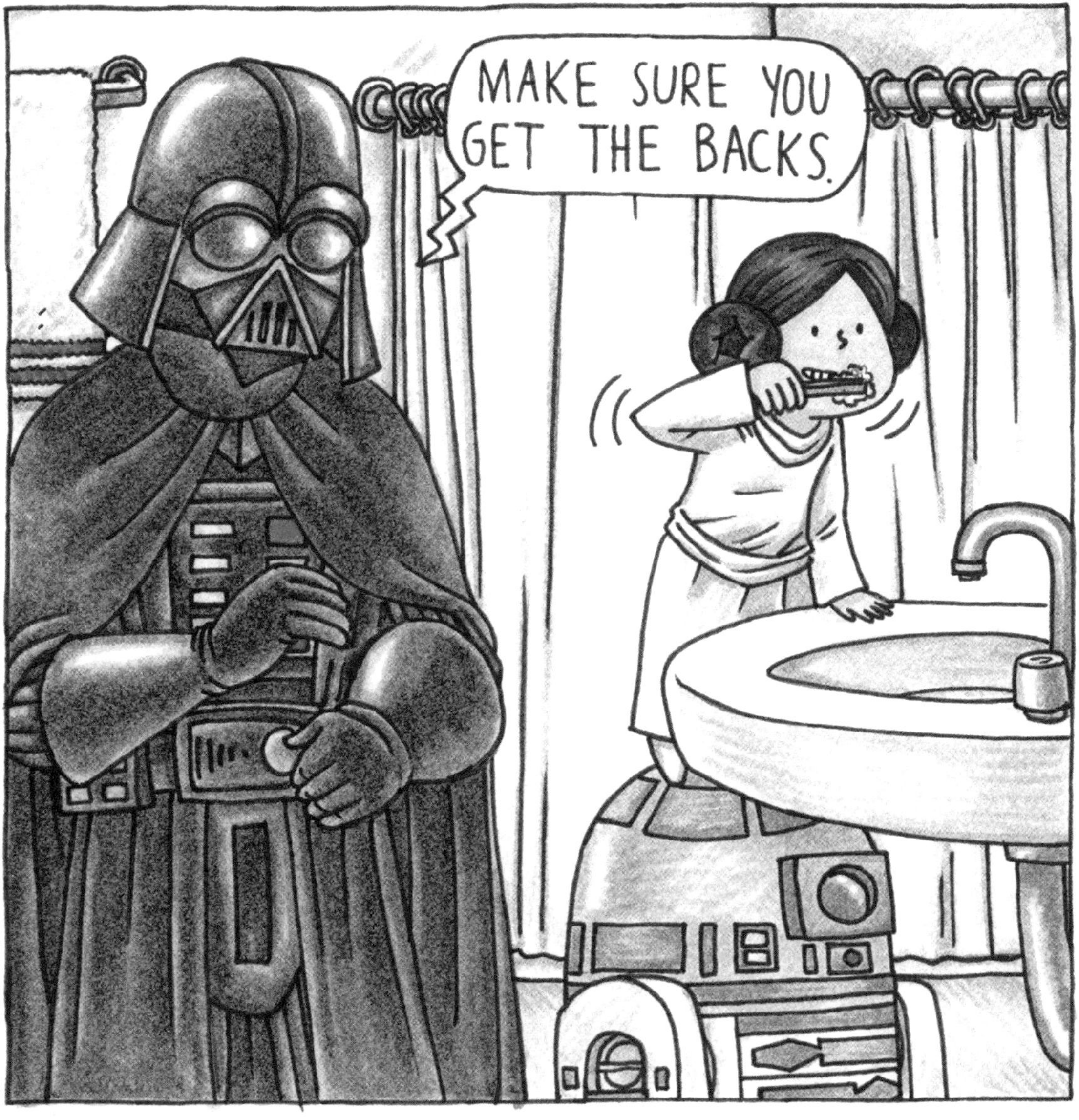
MAKE SURE YOU GET THE BACKS.

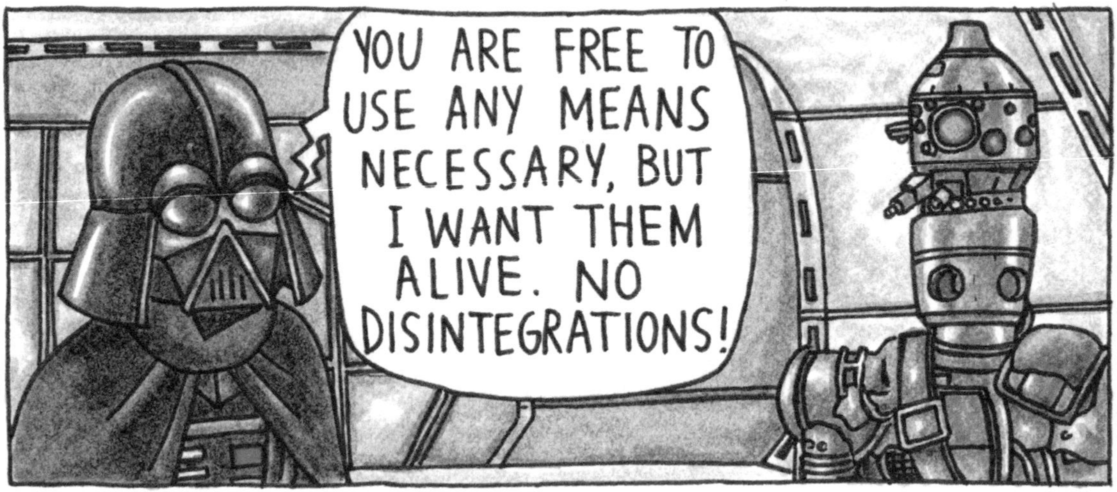
YOU ARE FREE TO USE ANY MEANS NECESSARY, BUT I WANT THEM ALIVE. NO DISINTEGRATIONS!

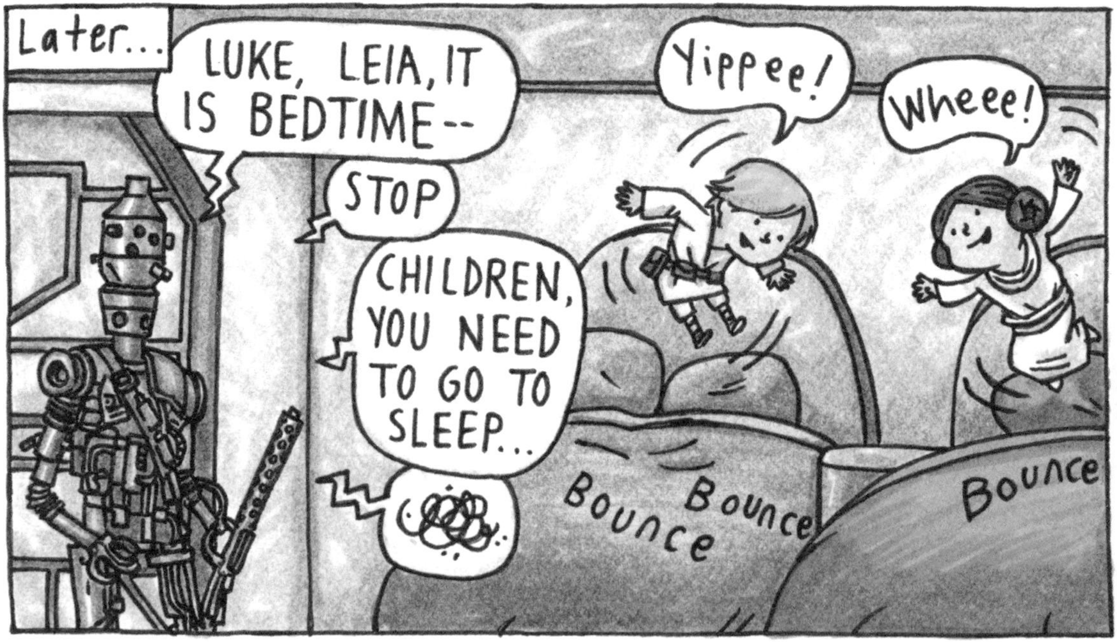
Later...
LUKE, LEIA, IT IS BEDTIME--
STOP
CHILDREN, YOU NEED TO GO TO SLEEP...
Yippee!
Wheee!
Bounce
Bounce
Bounce

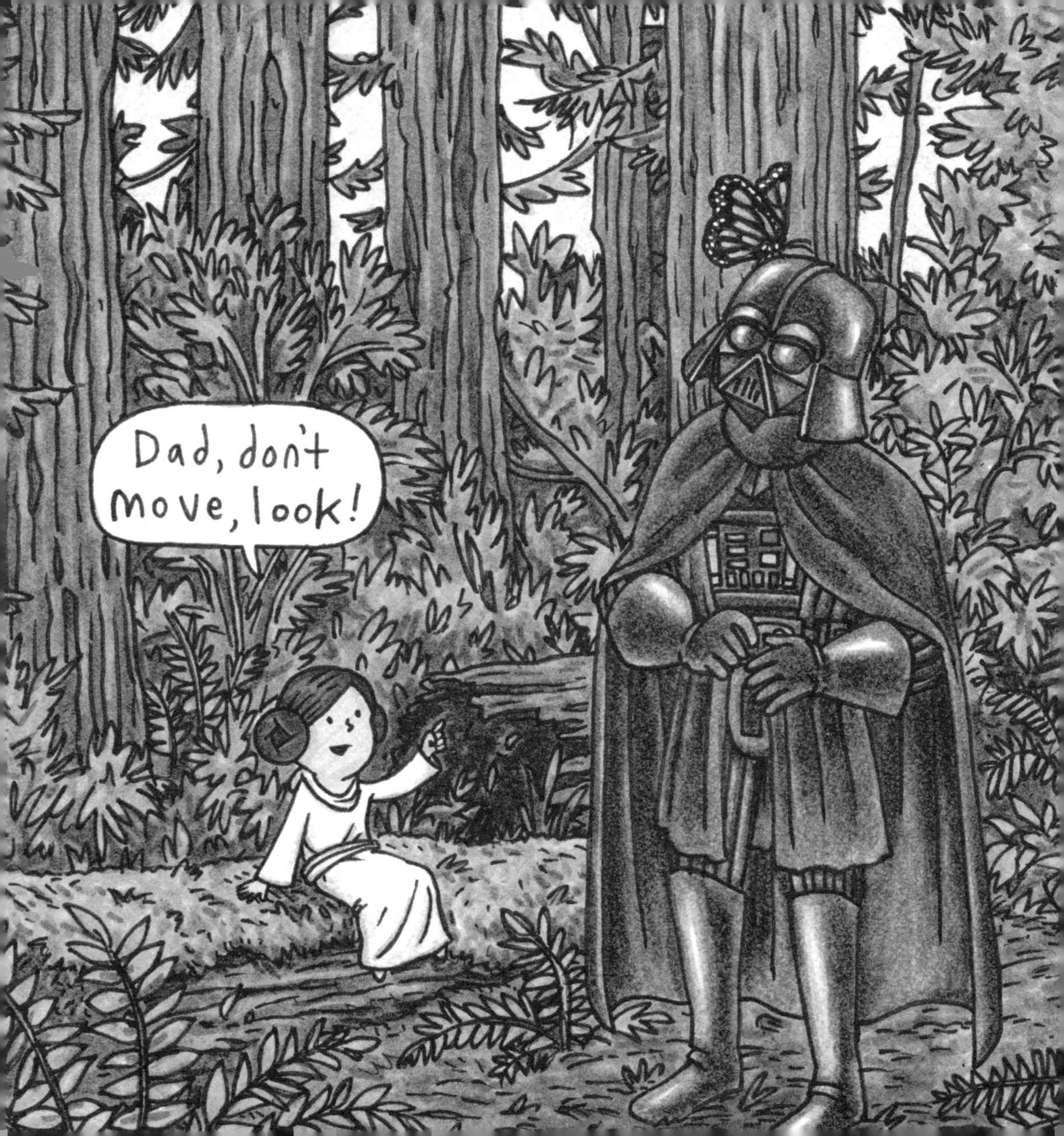
Dad, don't move, look!

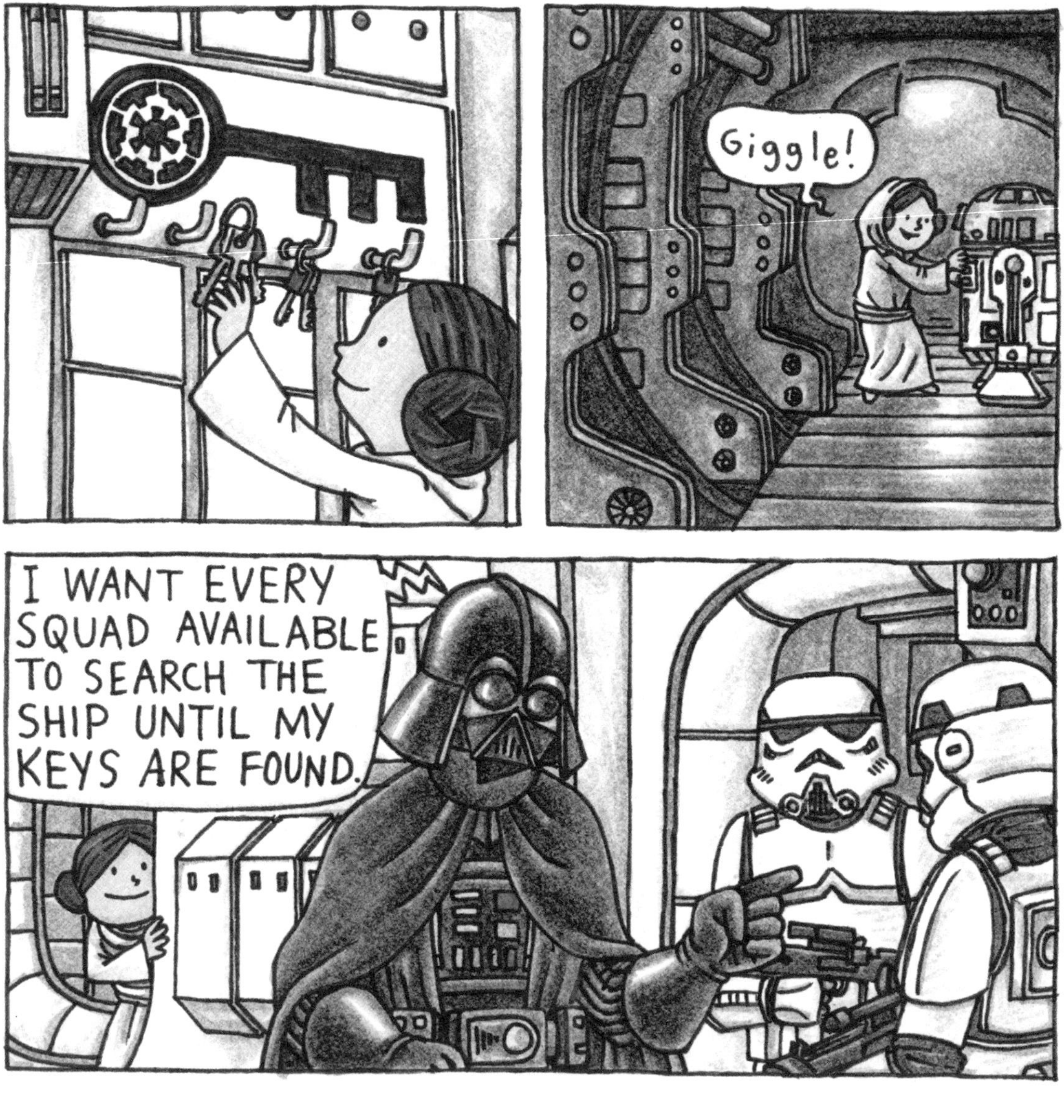
Giggle!
I WANT EVERY SQUAD AVAILABLE TO SEARCH THE SHIP UNTIL MY KEYS ARE FOUND.

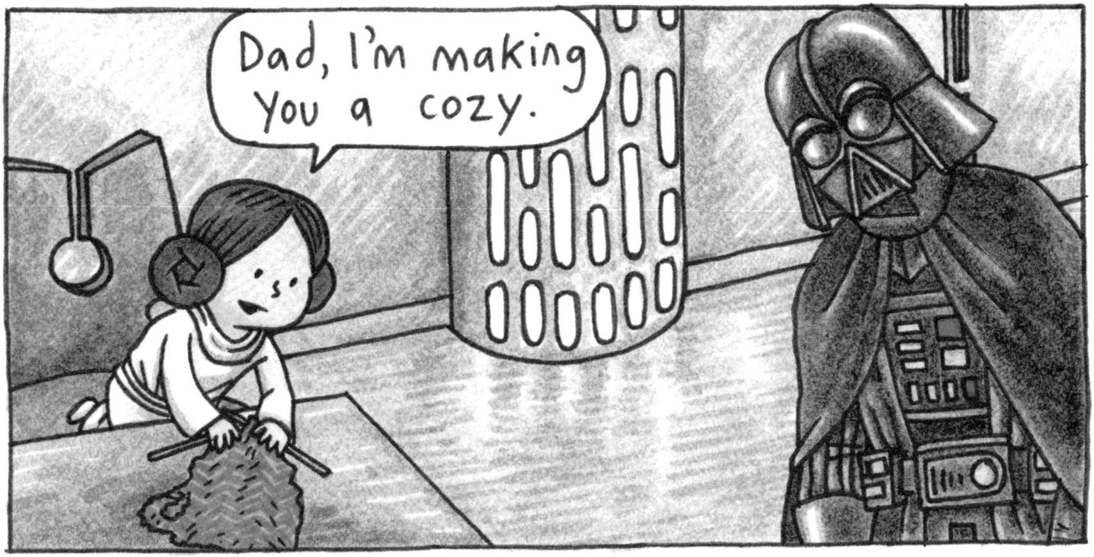
Dad, I'm making you a cozy.

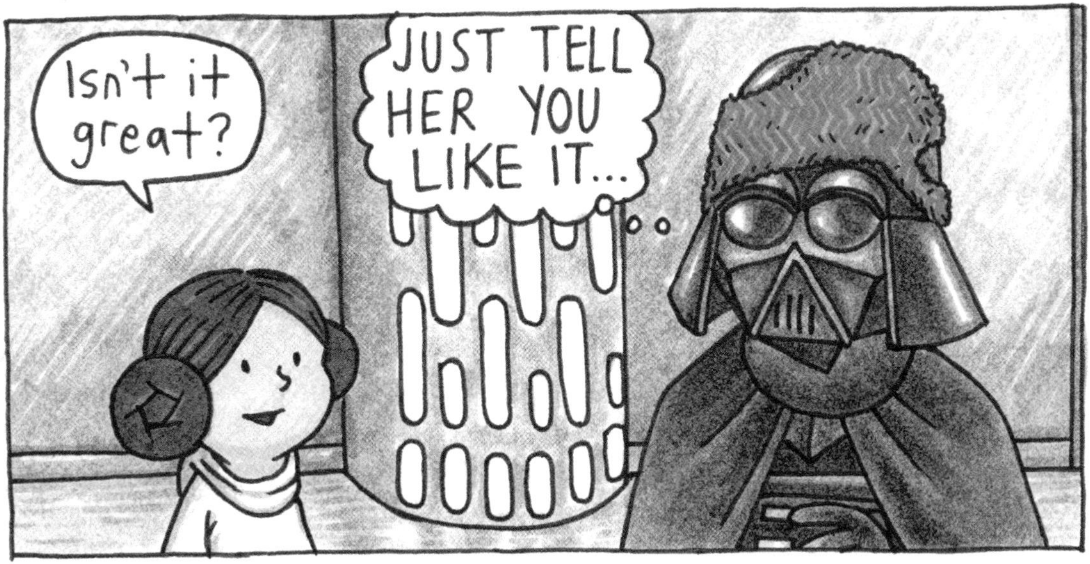
Isn't it great?
JUST TELL HER YOU LIKE IT...

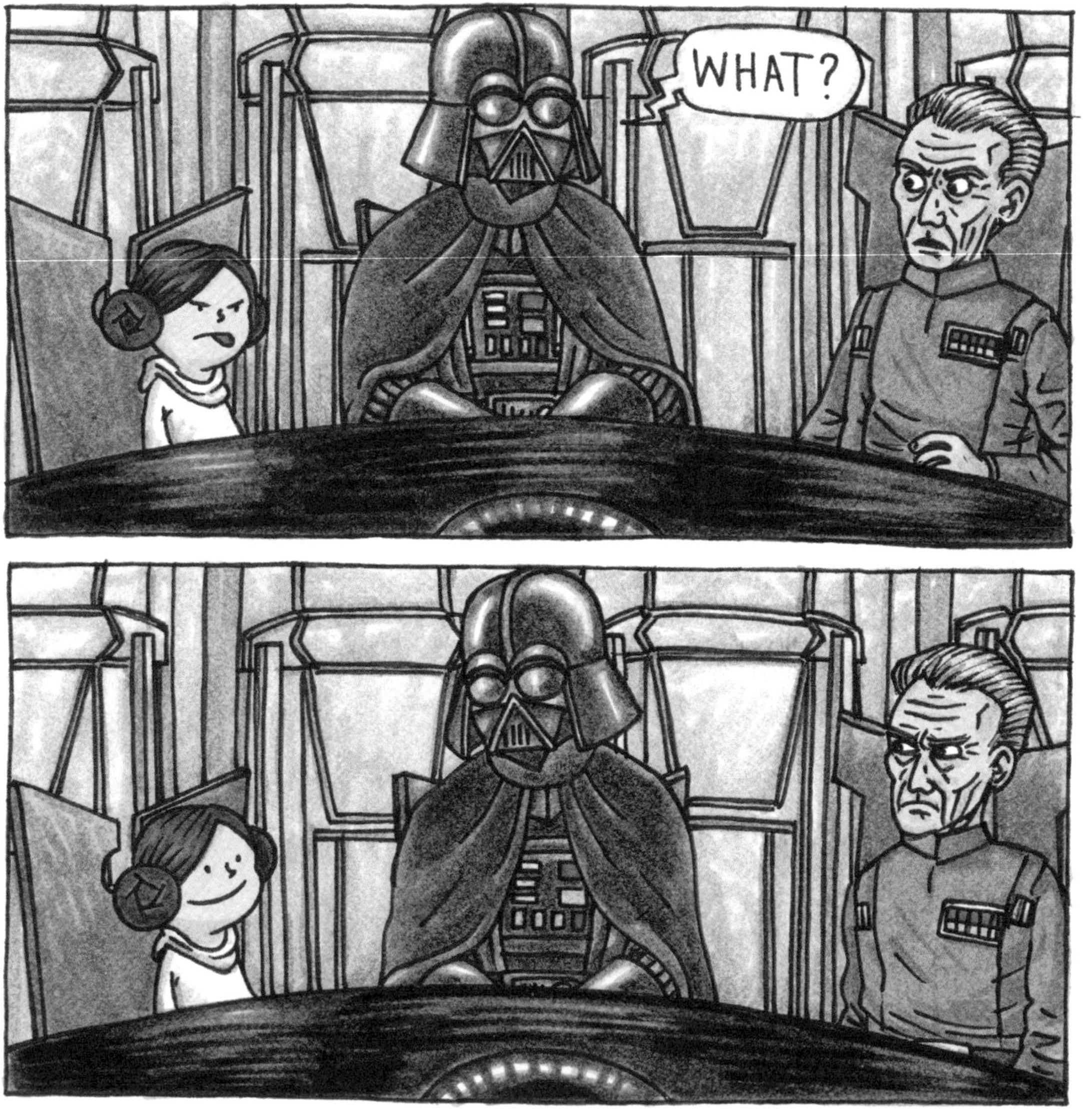
WHAT?

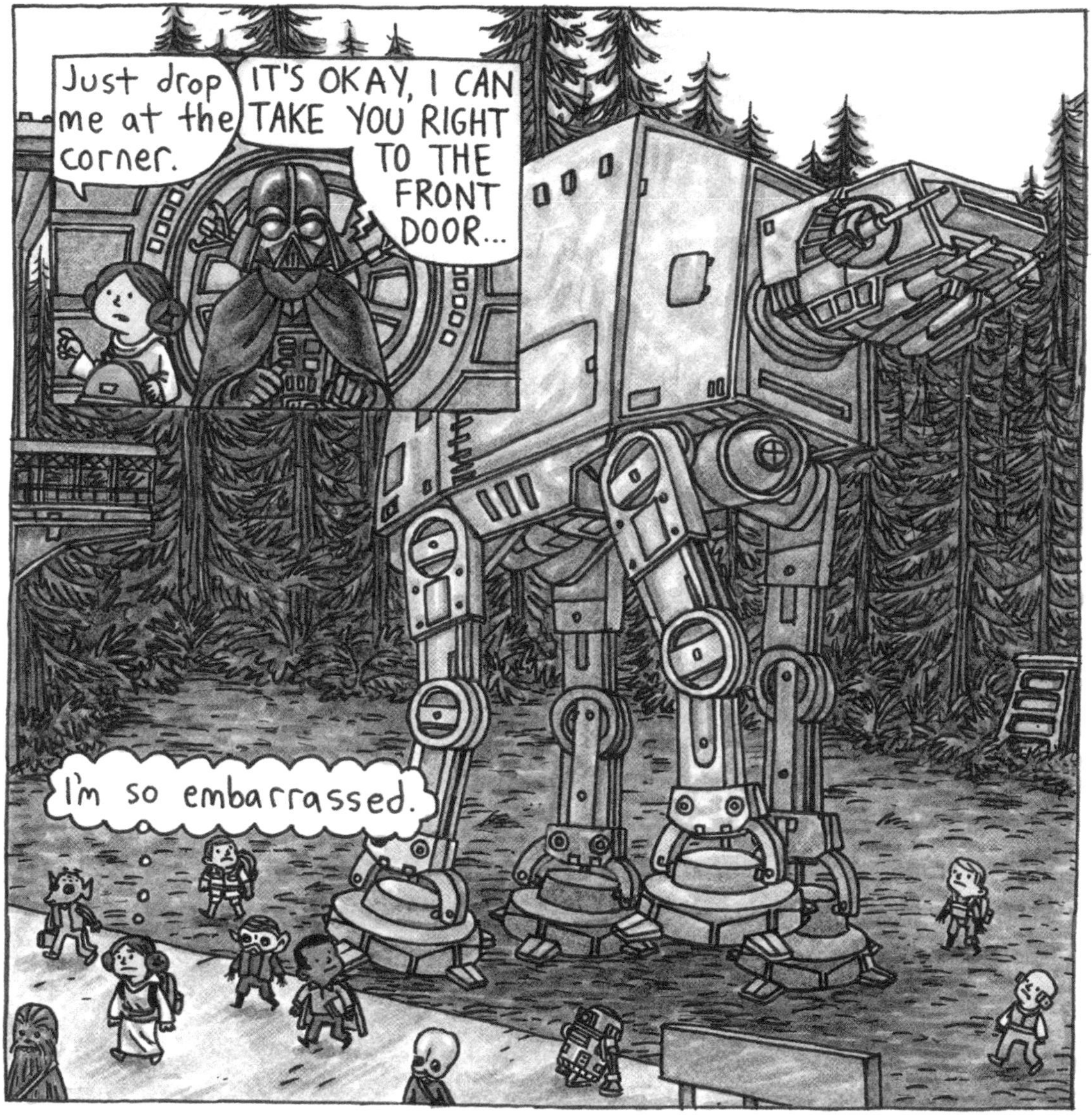
Just drop me at the corner.
IT'S OKAY, I CAN TAKE YOU RIGHT TO THE FRONT DOOR...
I'm so embarrassed.

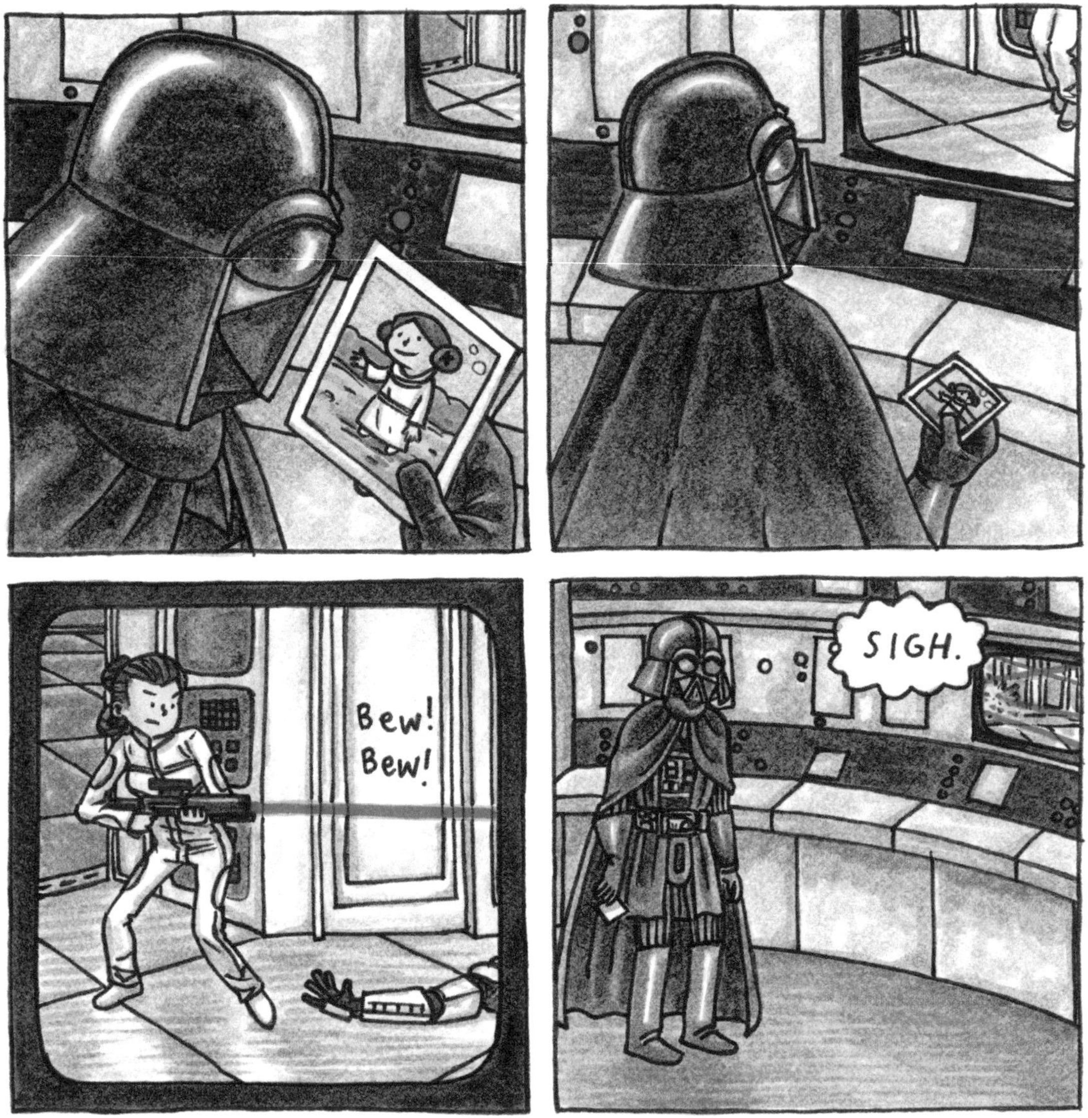
Bew!
Bew!
SIGH.

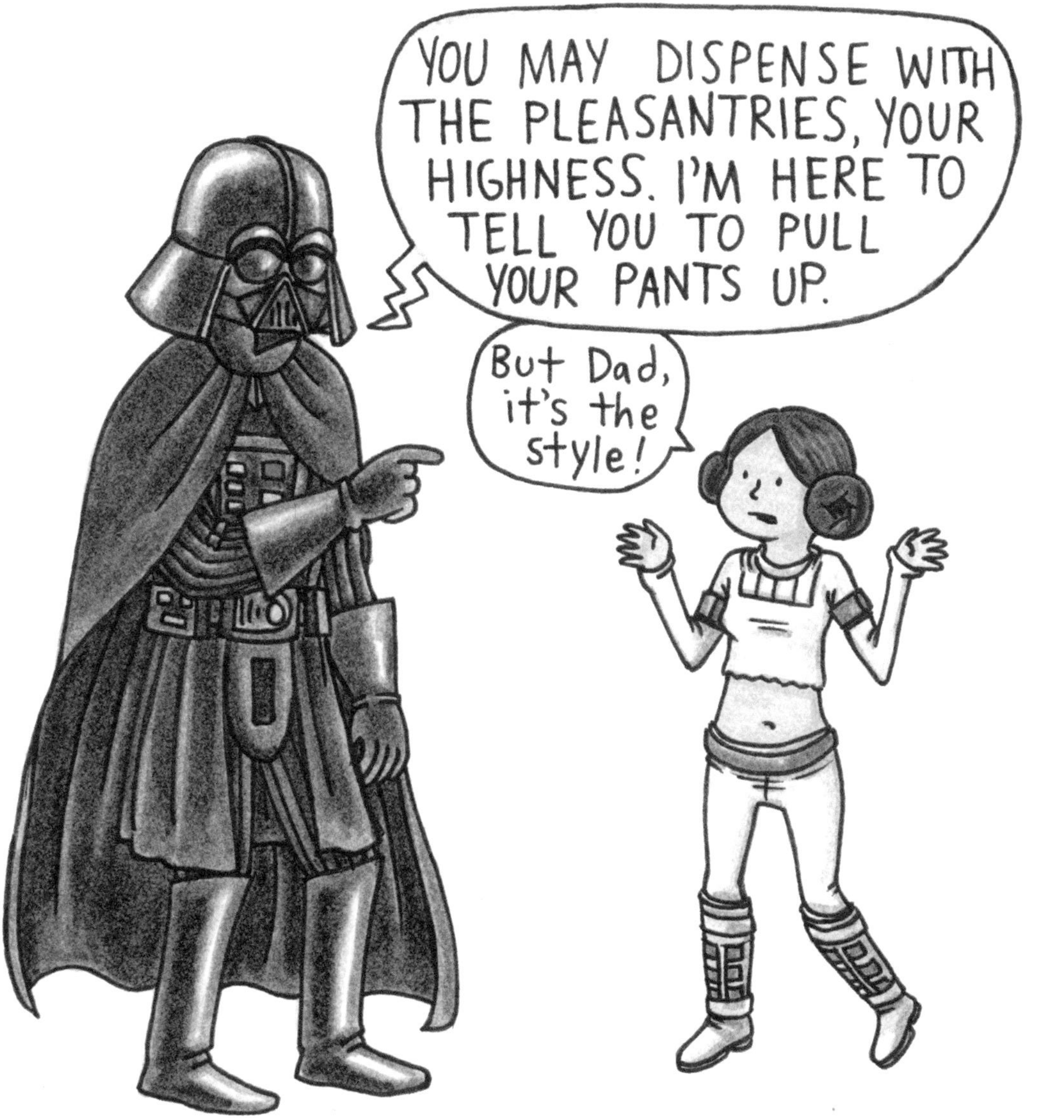
YOU MAY DISPENSE WITH THE PLEASANTRIES, YOUR HIGHNESS. I'M HERE TO TELL YOU TO PULL YOUR PANTS UP.
But Dad, it's the style!

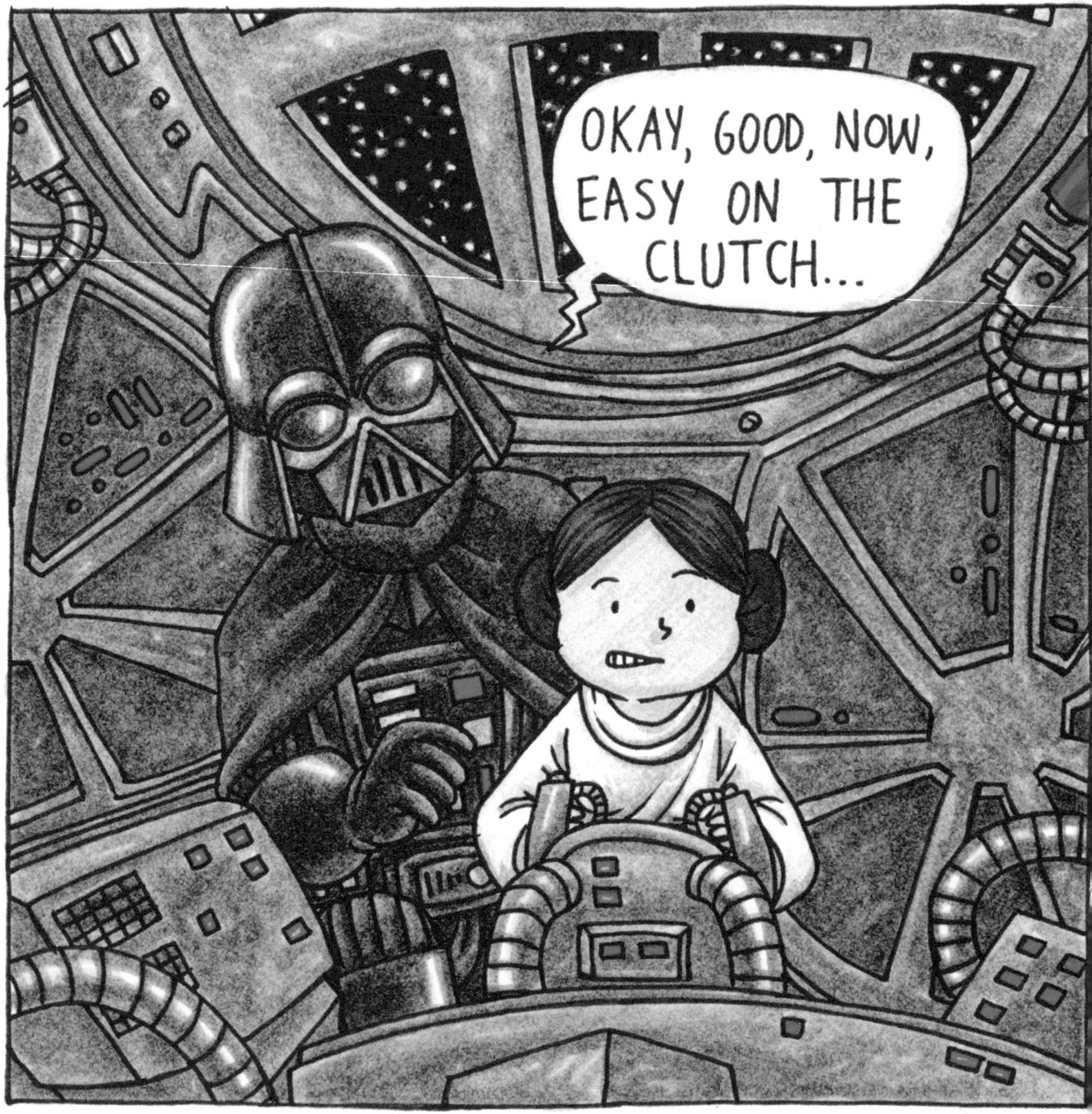
OKAY, GOOD, NOW, EASY ON THE CLUTCH...

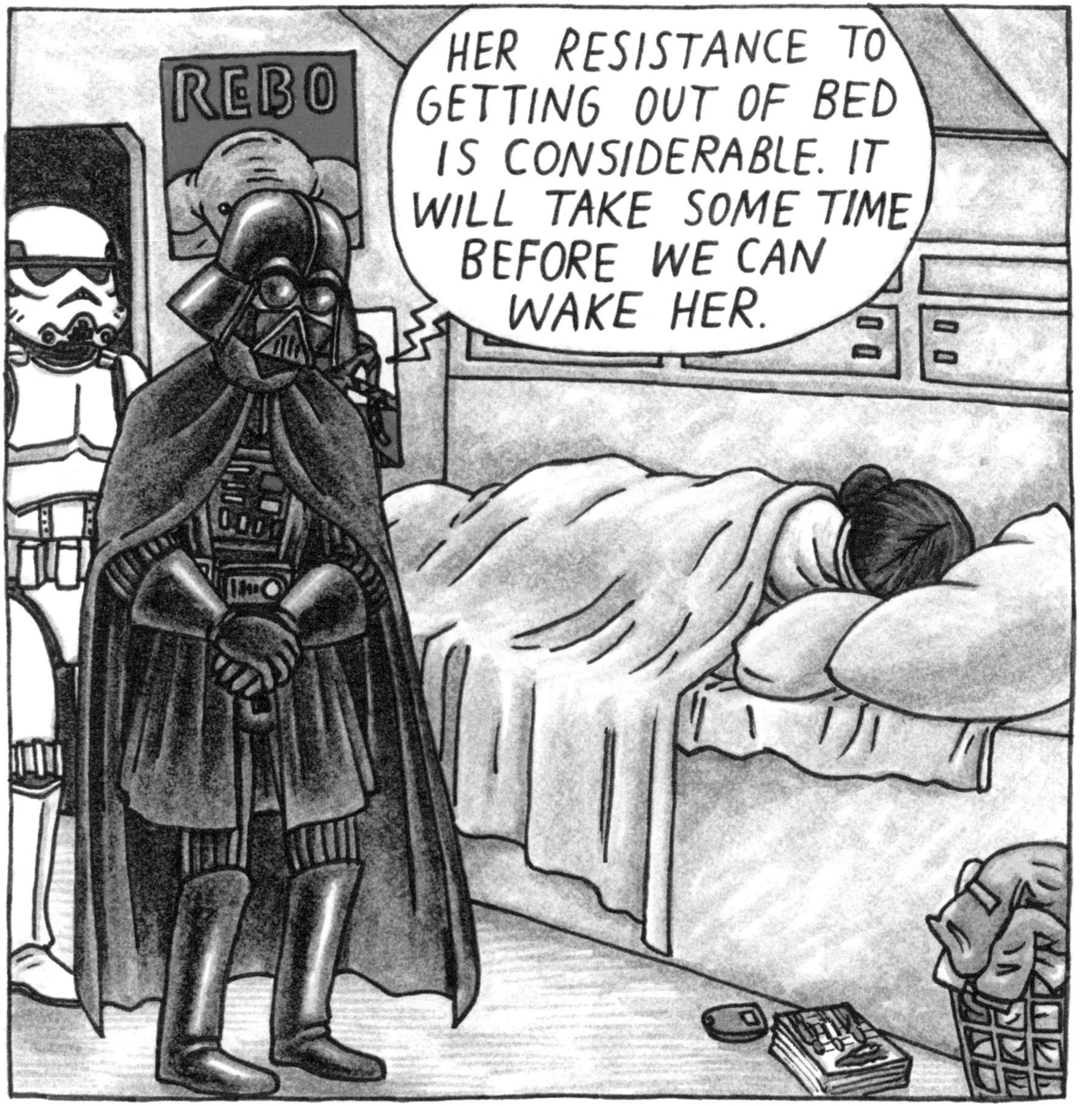
REBO
HER RESISTANCE TO GETTING OUT OF BED IS CONSIDERABLE. IT WILL TAKE SOME TIME BEFORE WE CAN WAKE HER.

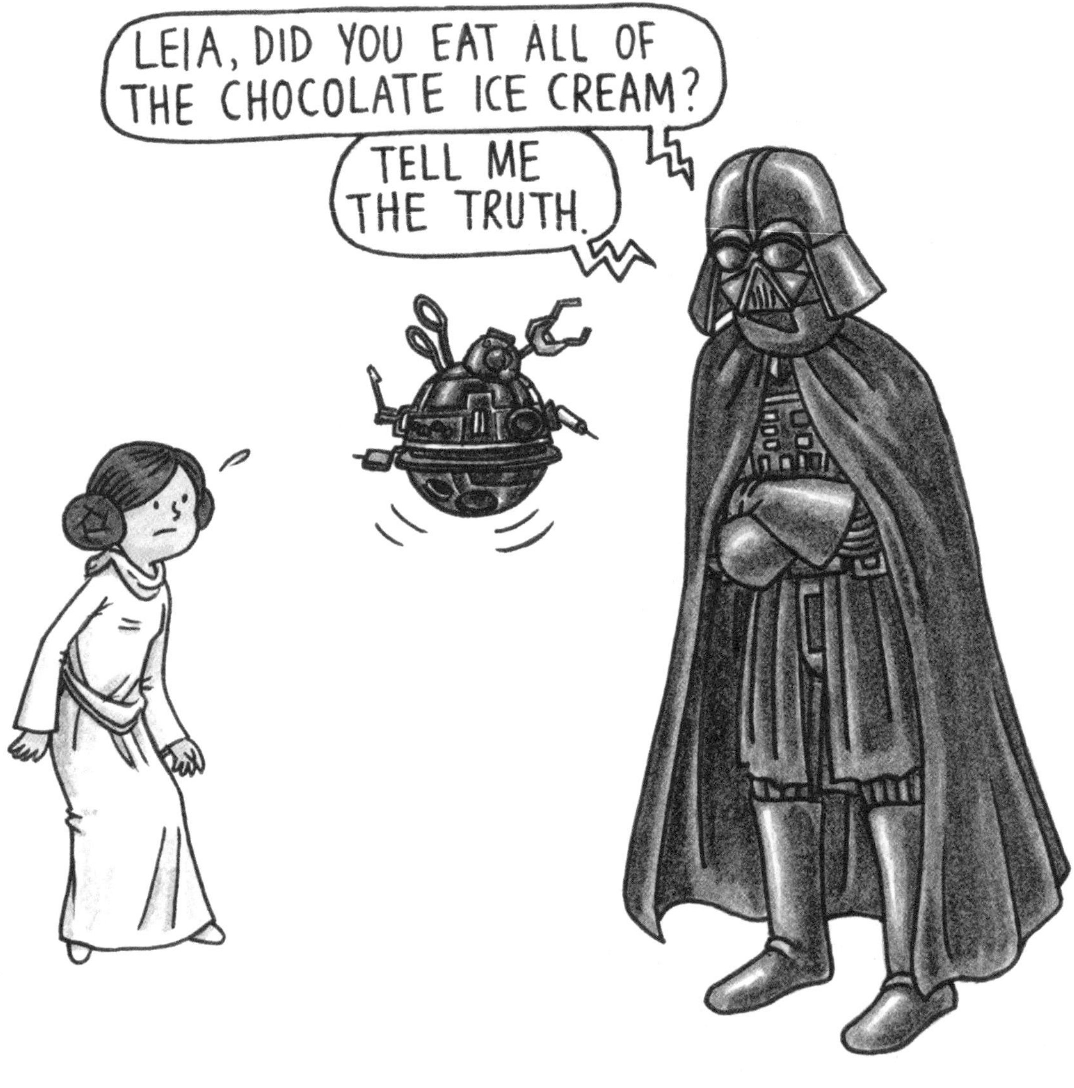
LEIA, DID YOU EAT ALL OF THE CHOCOLATE ICE CREAM?
TELL ME THE TRUTH.

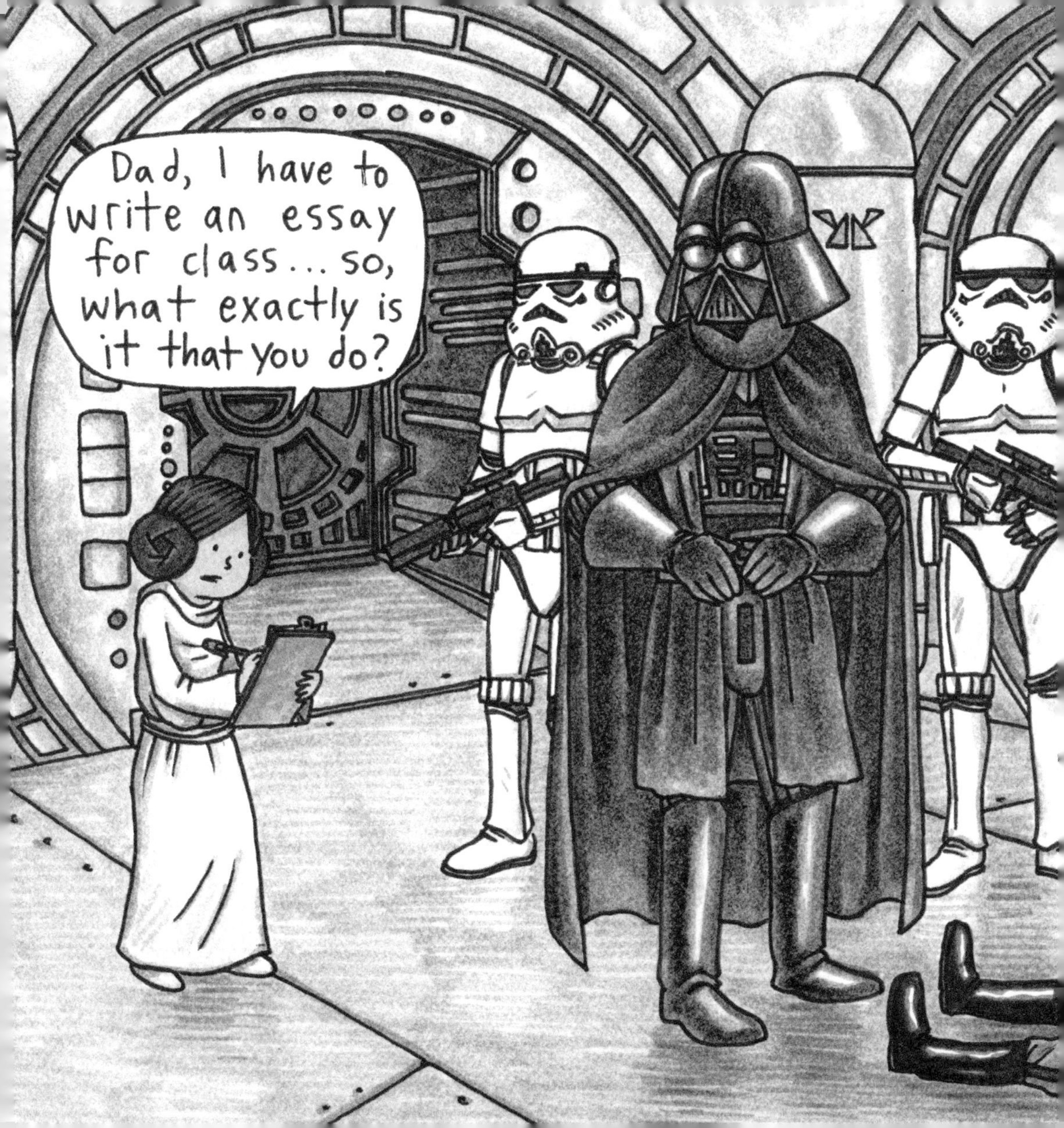
Dad, I have to write an essay for class... so, what exactly is it that you do?

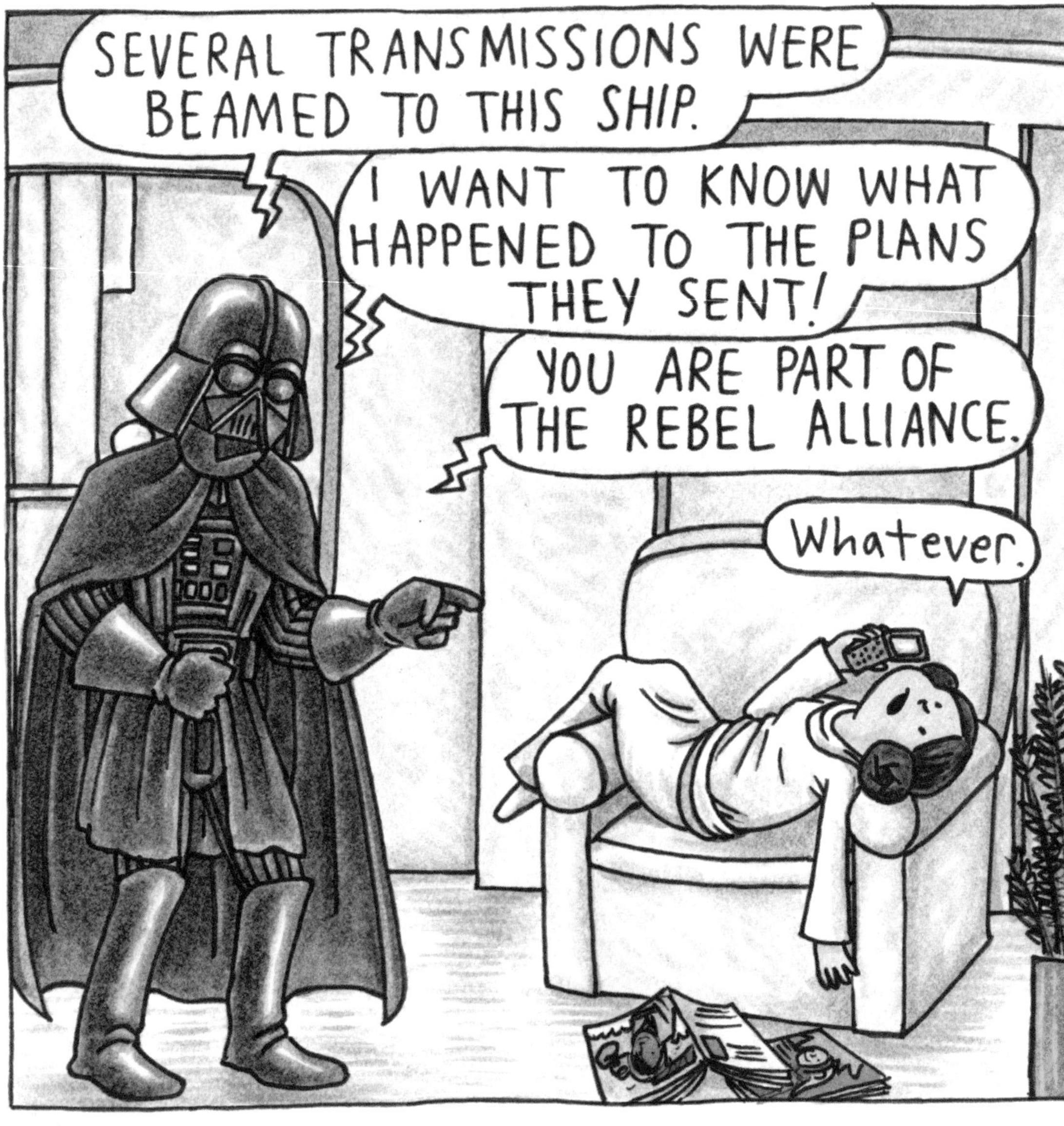
SEVERAL TRANSMISSIONS WERE BEAMED TO THIS SHIP.
I WANT TO KNOW WHAT HAPPENED TO THE PLANS THEY SENT!
YOU ARE PART OF THE REBEL ALLIANCE.
Whatever.

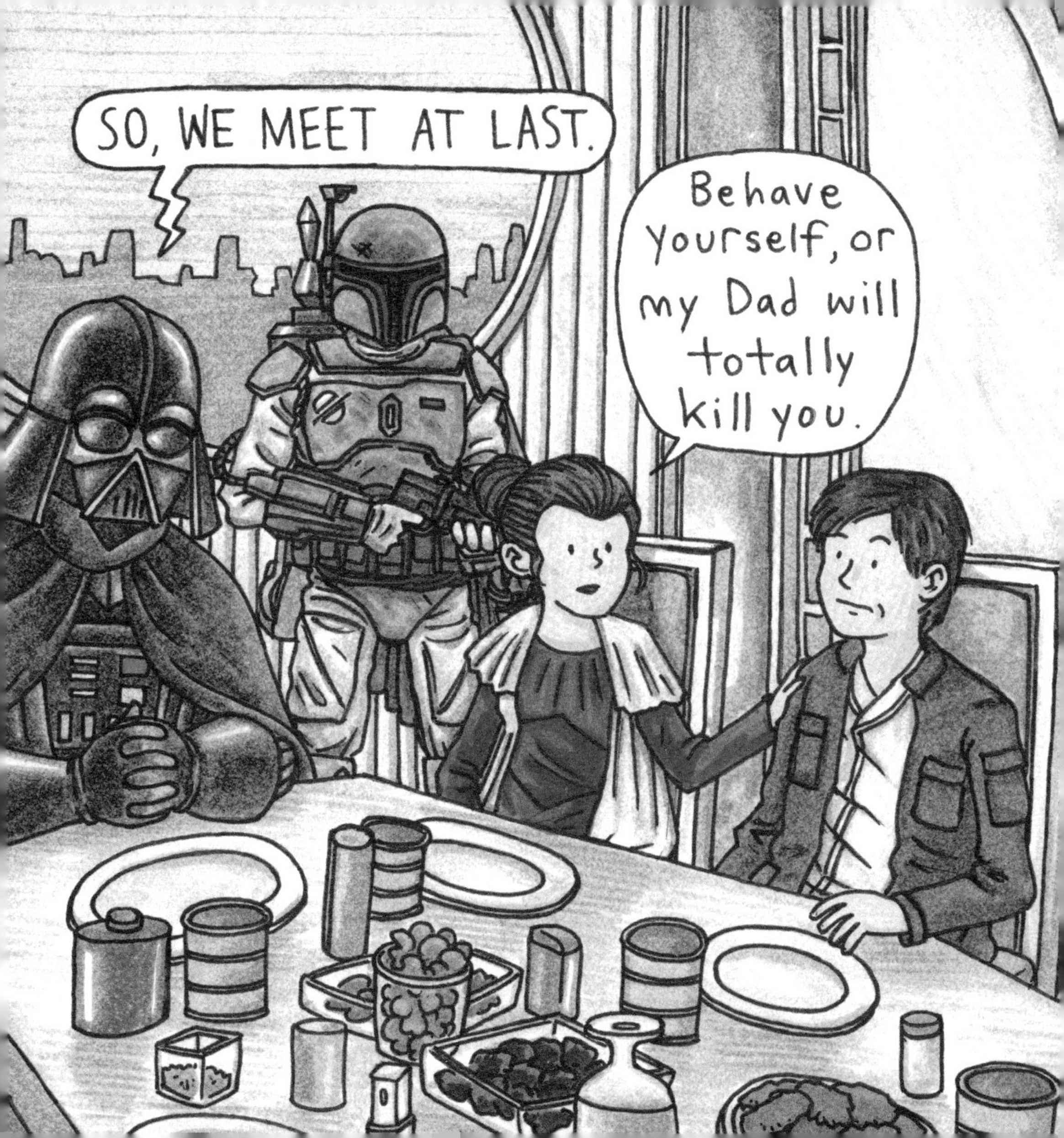
SO, WE MEET AT LAST.
Behave yourself, or my Dad will totally kill you.

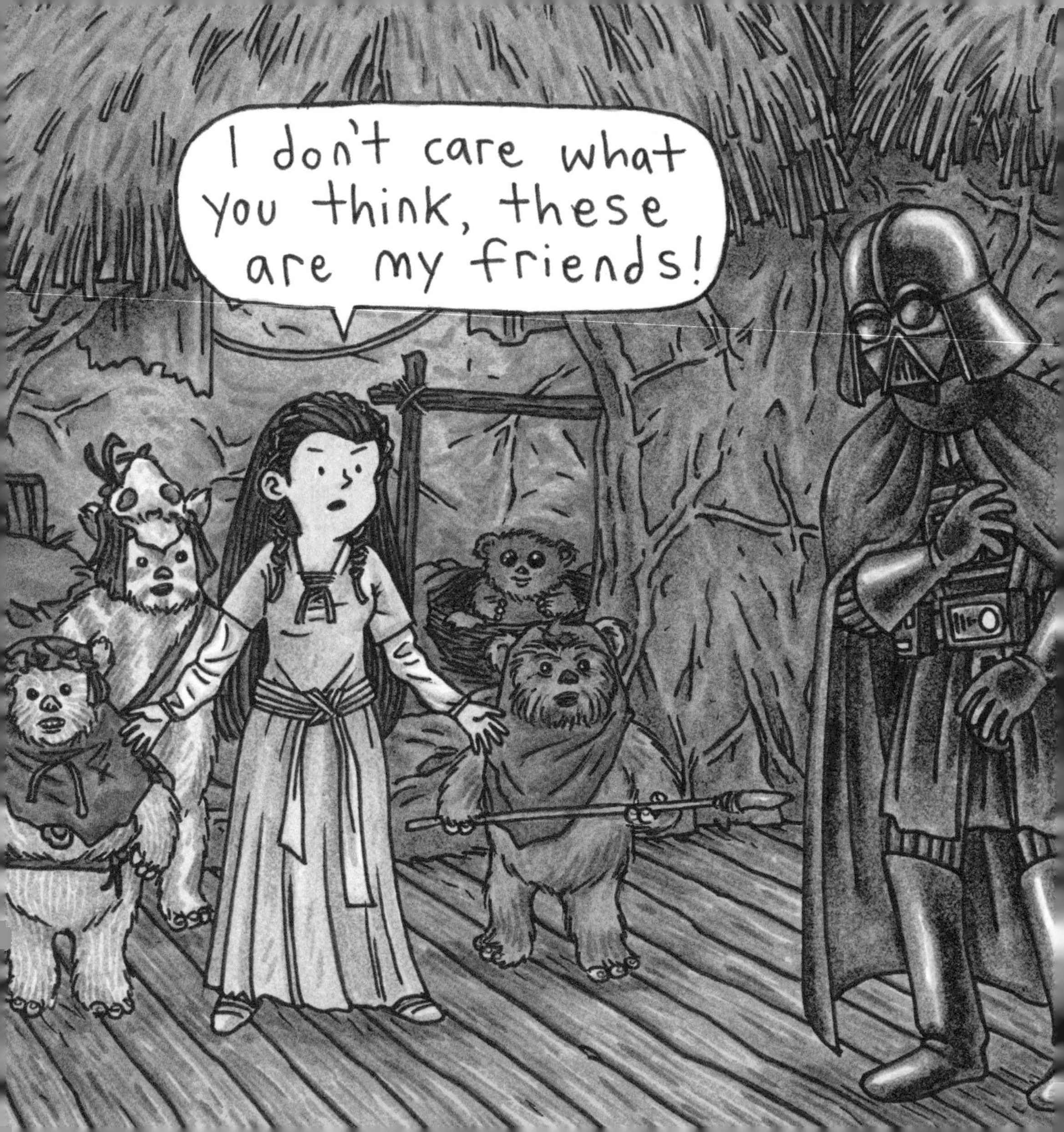
I don't care what you think, these are my friends!

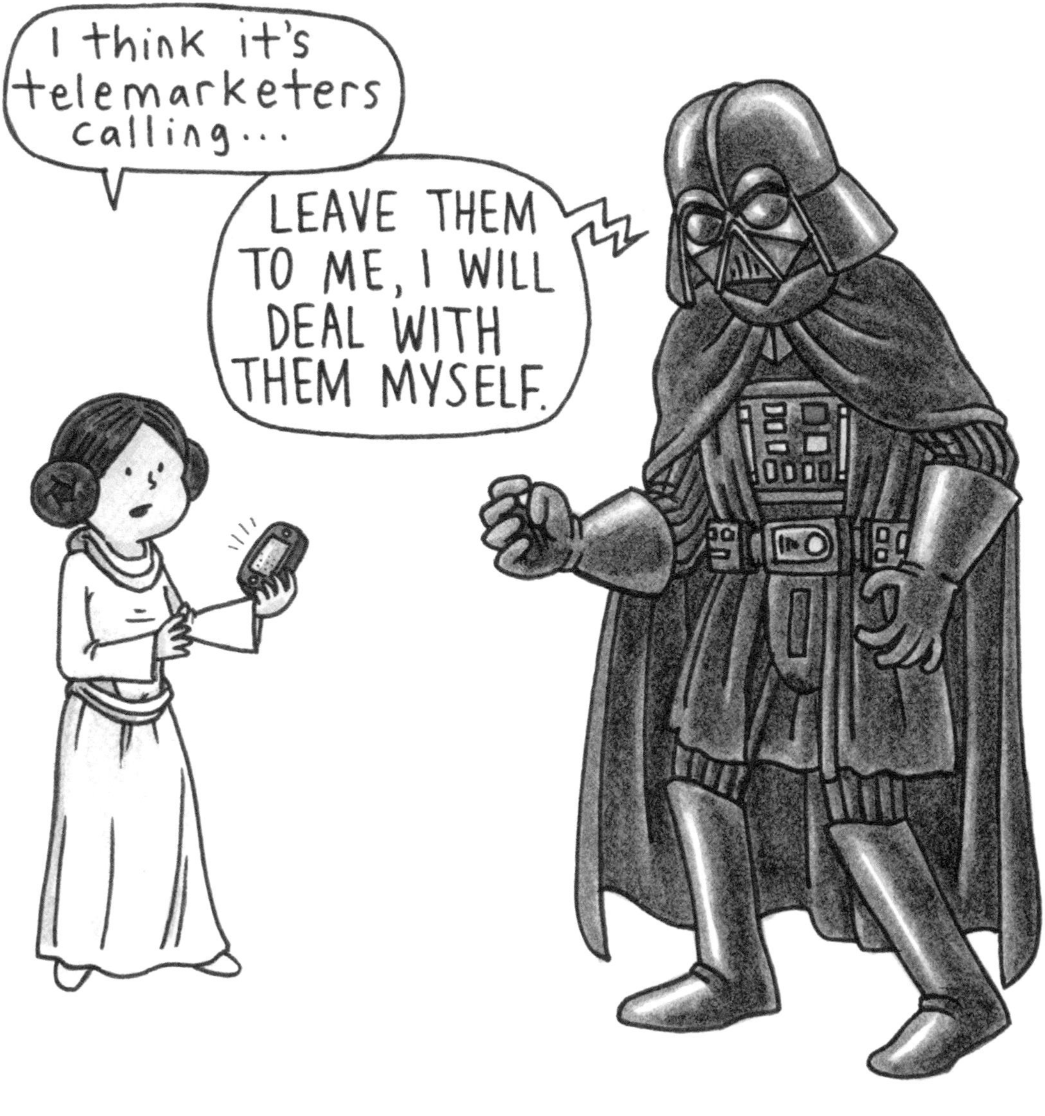
I think it's telemarketers calling...
LEAVE THEM TO ME, I WILL DEAL WITH THEM MYSELF.

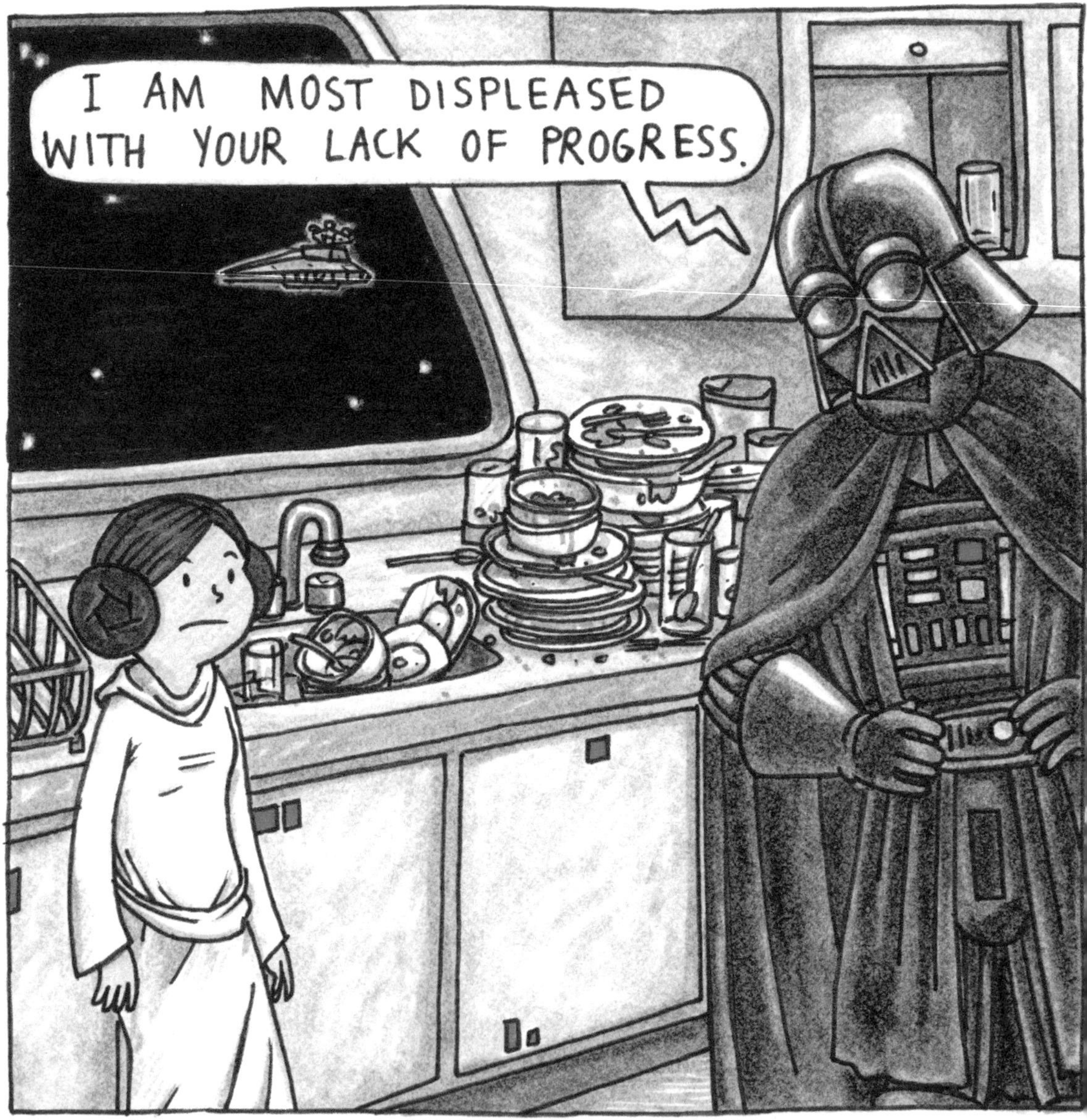
I AM MOST DISPLEASED WITH YOUR LACK OF PROGRESS.

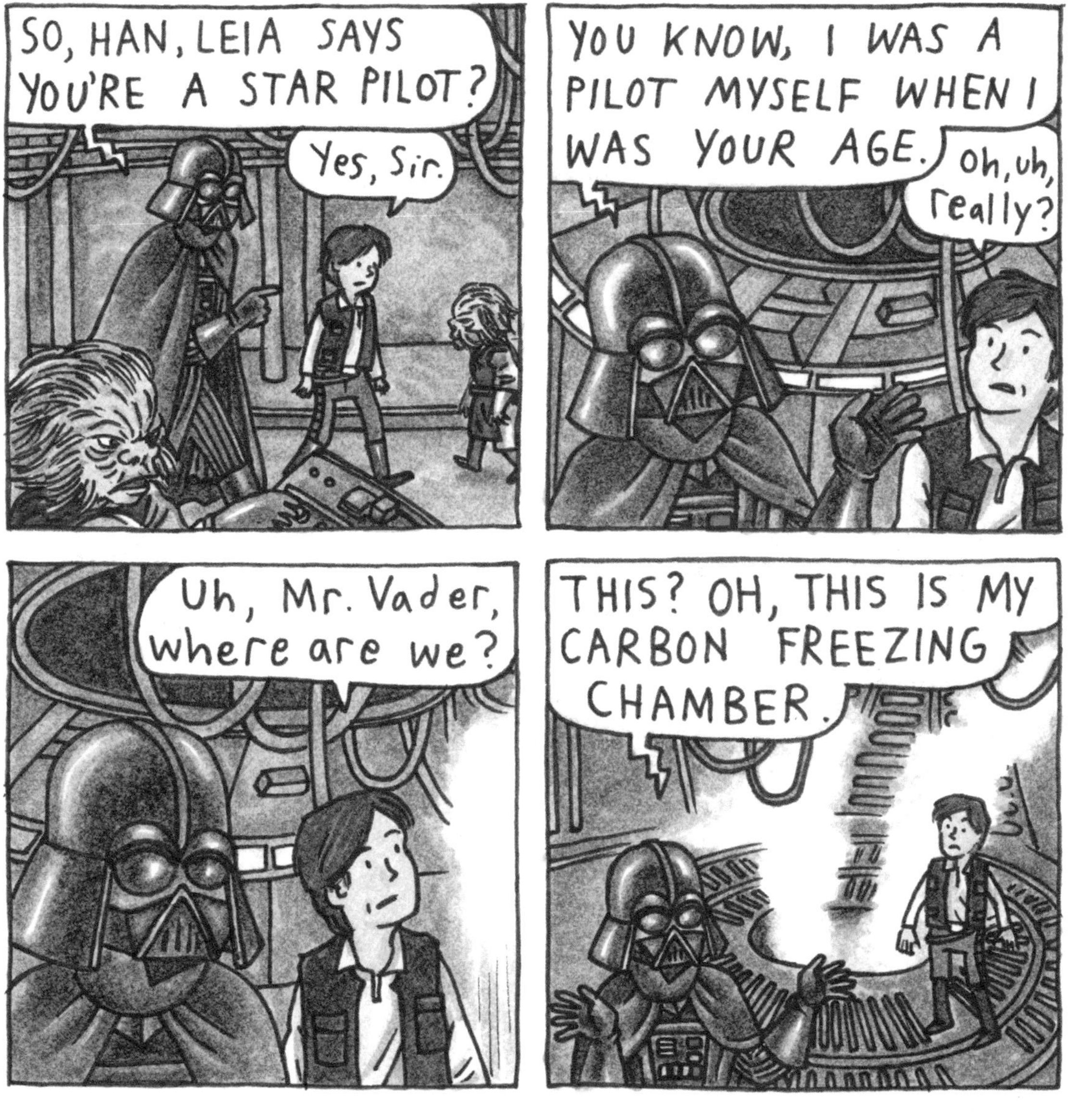
SO, HAN, LEIA SAYS YOU'RE A STAR PILOT?
Yes, Sir.
YOU KNOW, I WAS A PILOT MYSELF WHEN I WAS YOUR AGE.
Oh, uh, really?
Uh, Mr. Vader, where are we?
THIS? OH, THIS IS MY CARBON FREEZING CHAMBER.

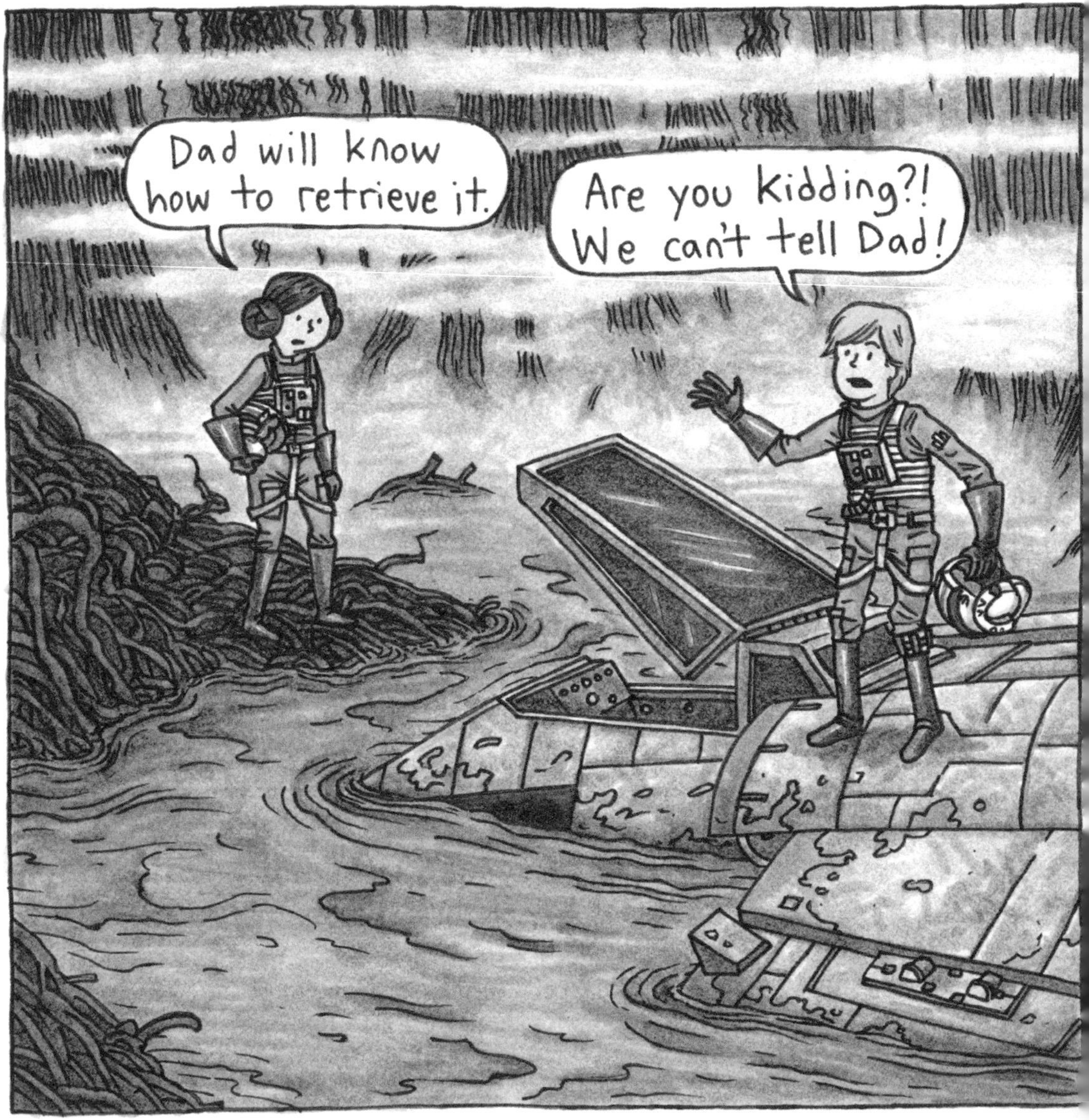
Dad will know how to retrieve it.
Are you kidding?! We can't tell Dad!

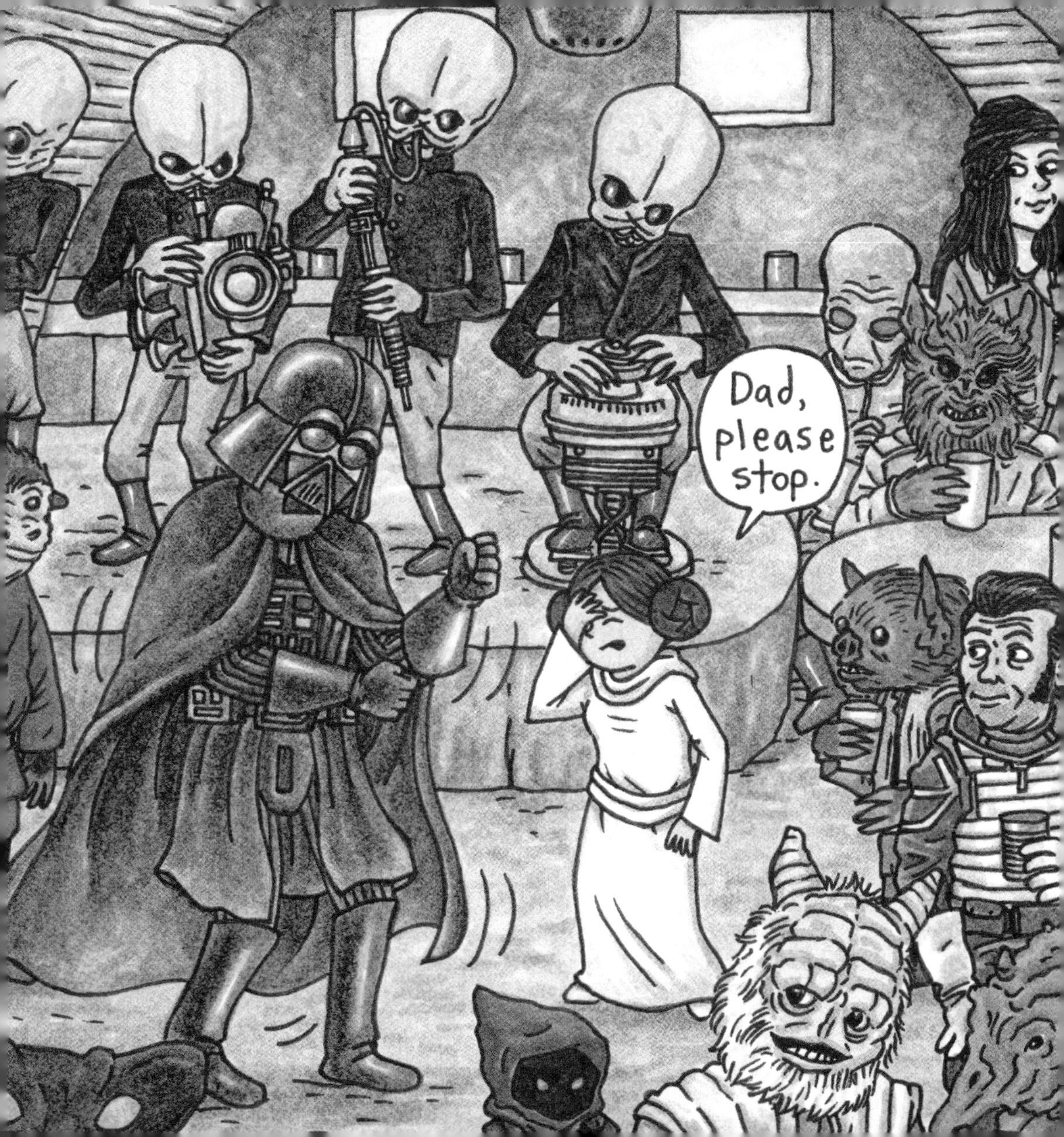
Dad, please stop.

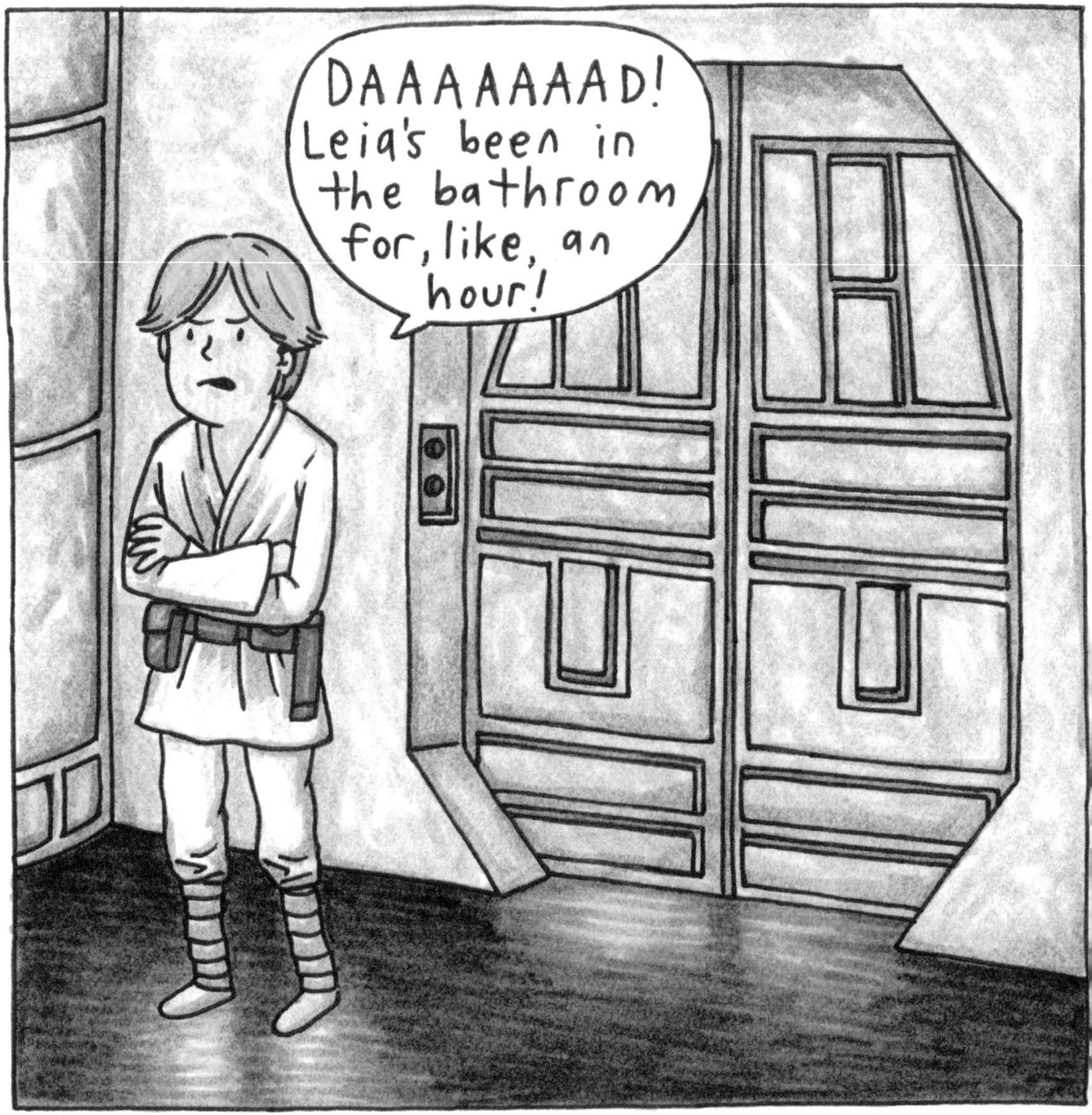
DAAAAAAAD! Leia's been in the bathroom for, like, an hour!

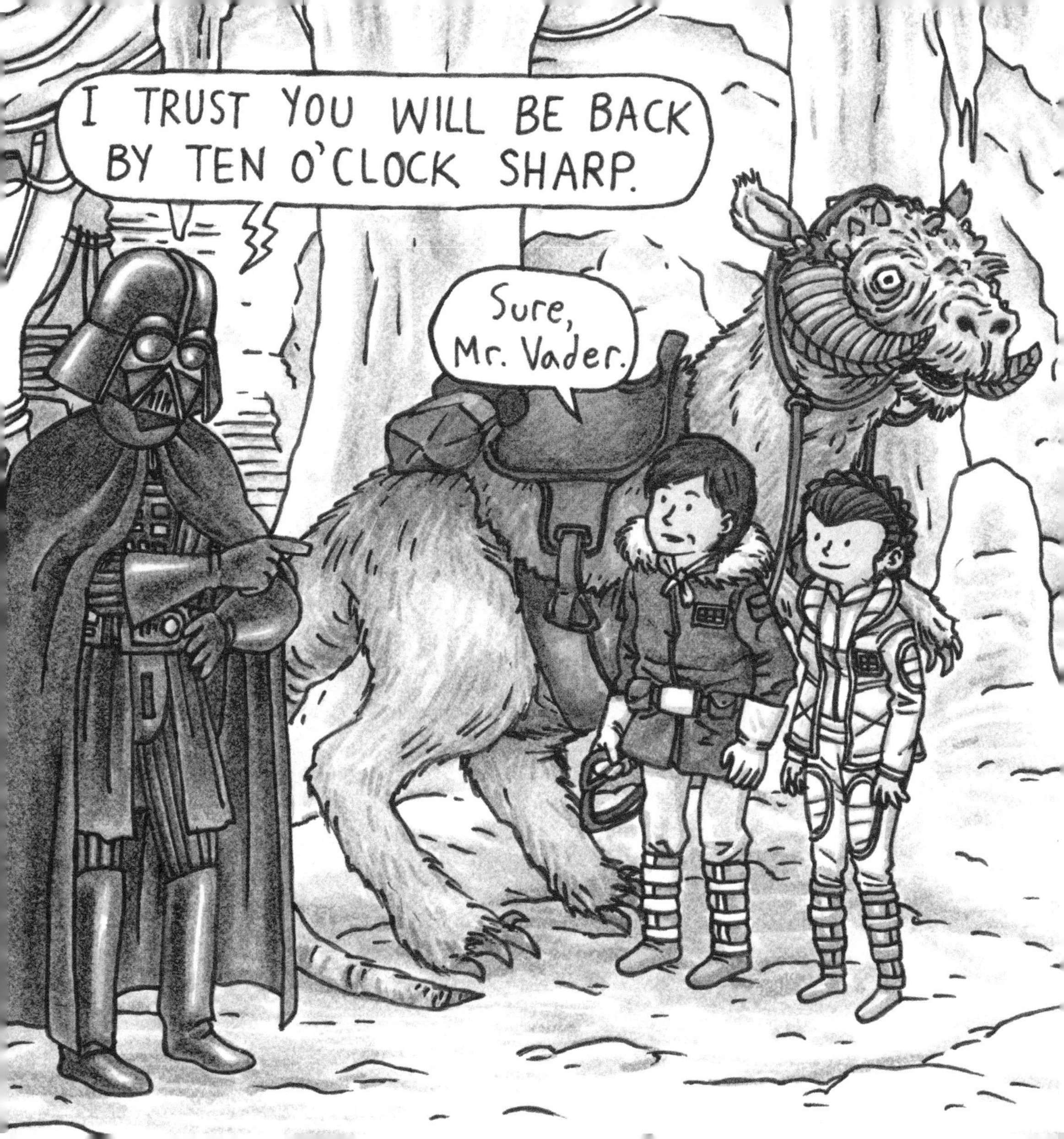
I TRUST YOU WILL BE BACK BY TEN O'CLOCK SHARP.
Sure, Mr. Vader.

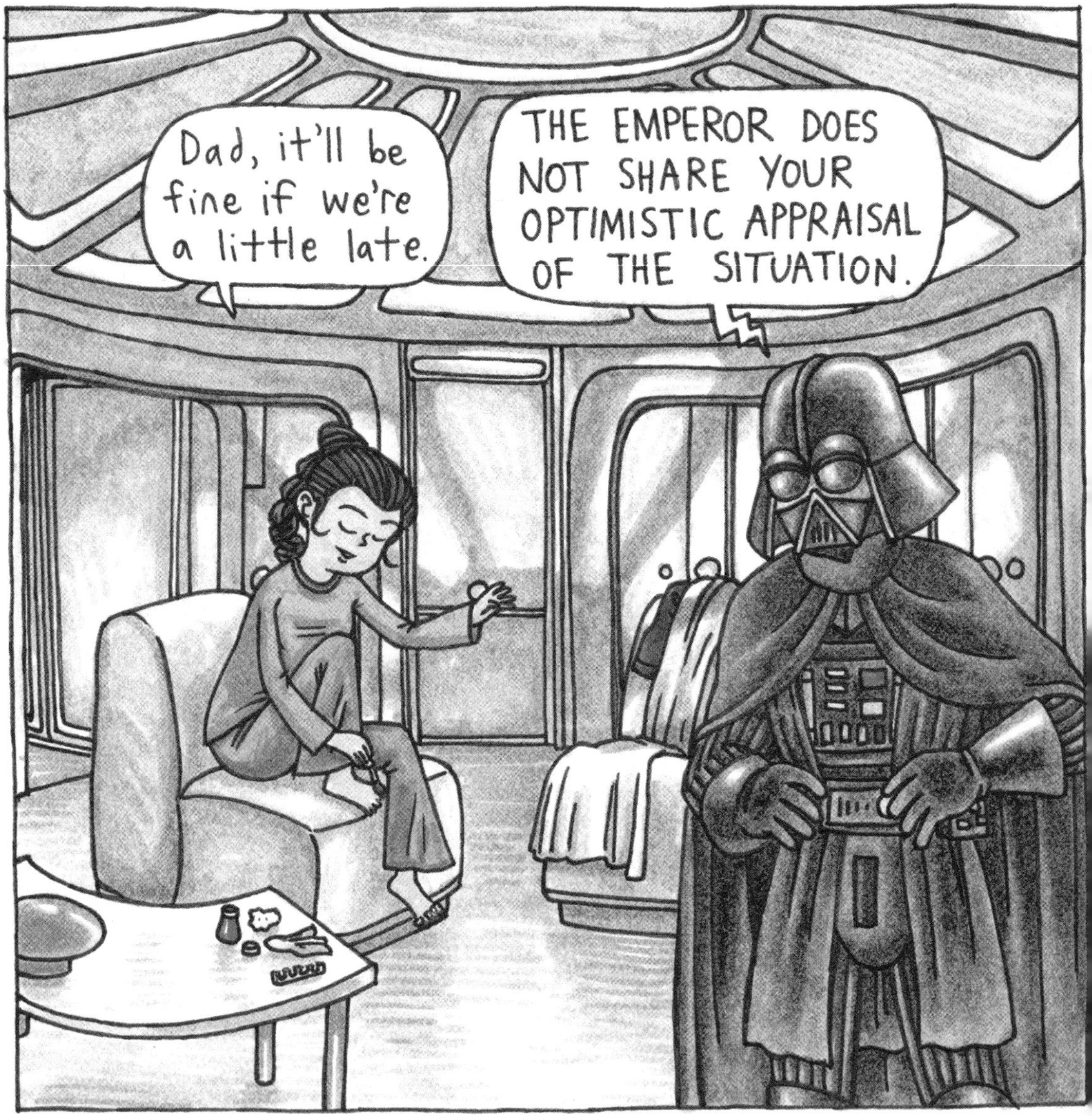
Dad, it'll be fine if we're a little late.
THE EMPEROR DOES NOT SHARE YOUR OPTIMISTIC APPRAISAL OF THE SITUATION.

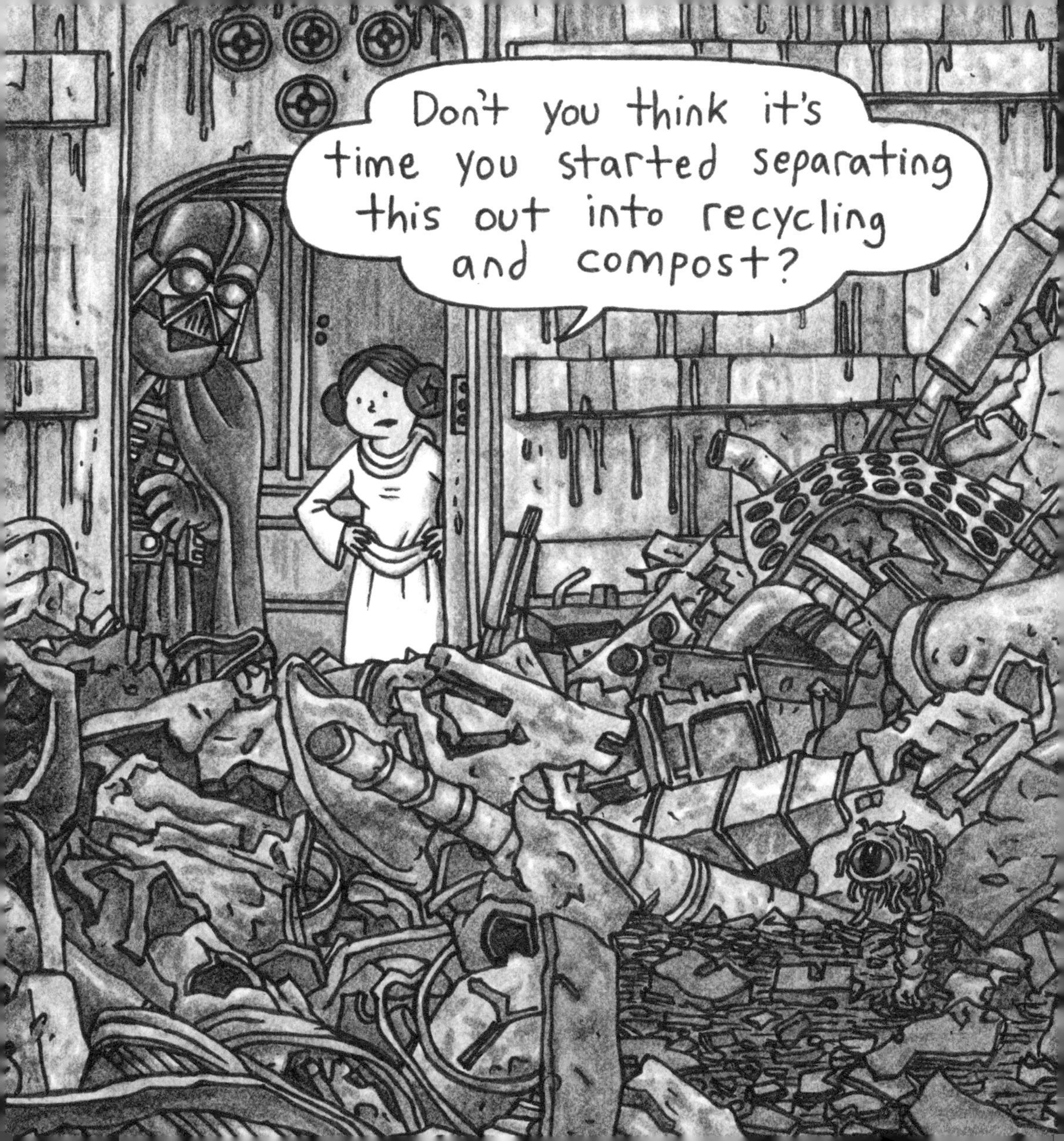
Don't you think it's time you started separating this out into recycling and compost?

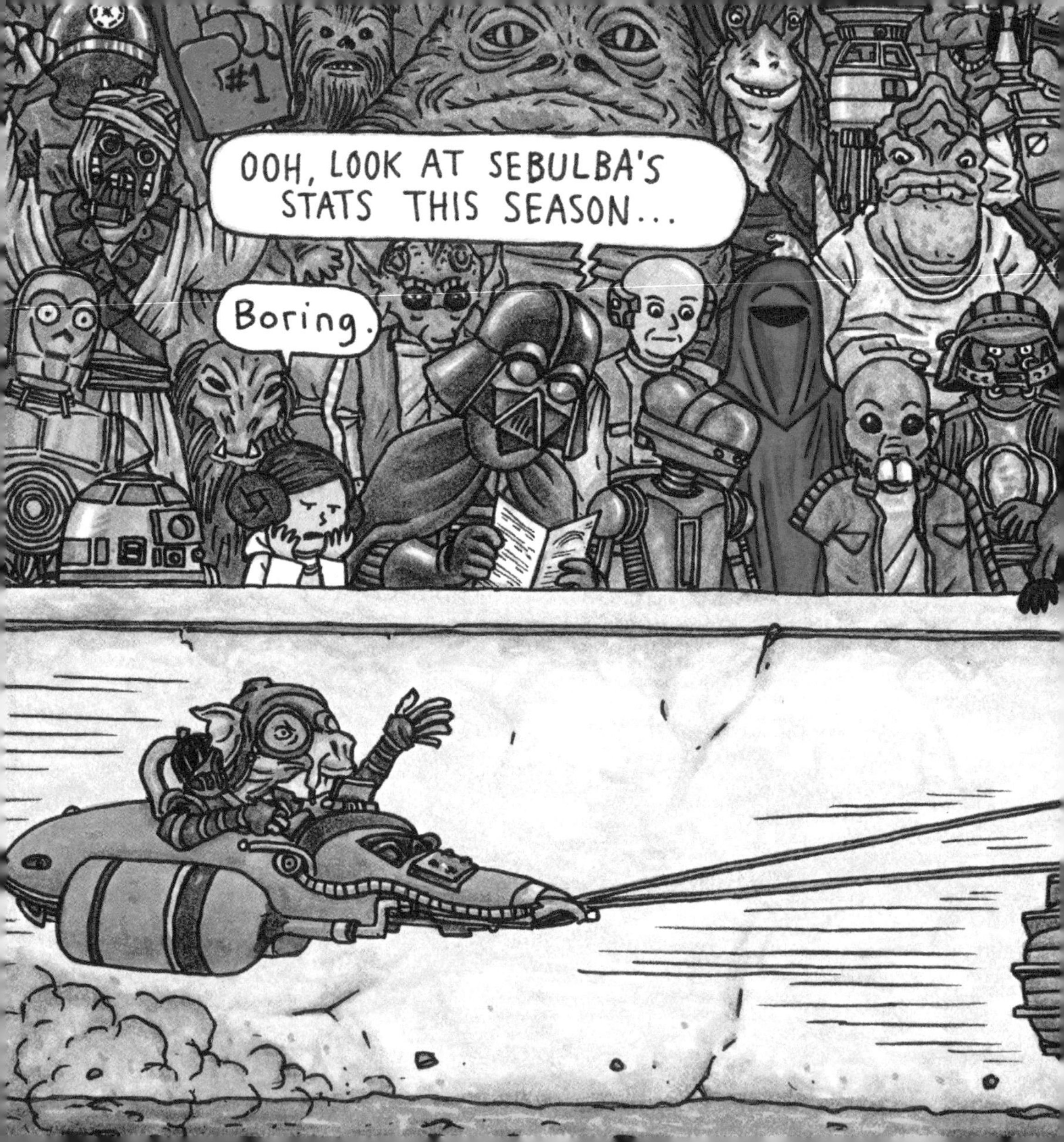
OOH, LOOK AT SEBULBA'S STATS THIS SEASON...
Boring.
#1

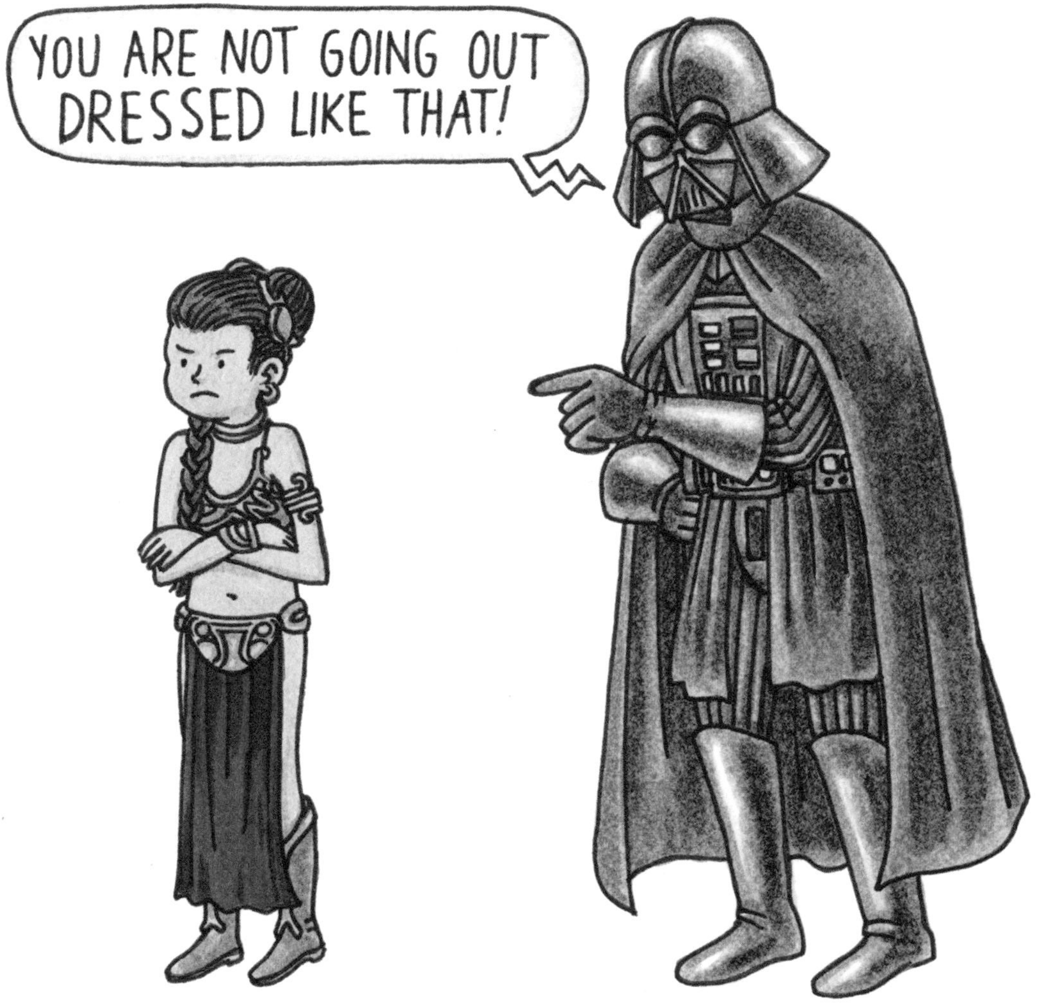
YOU ARE NOT GOING OUT DRESSED LIKE THAT!

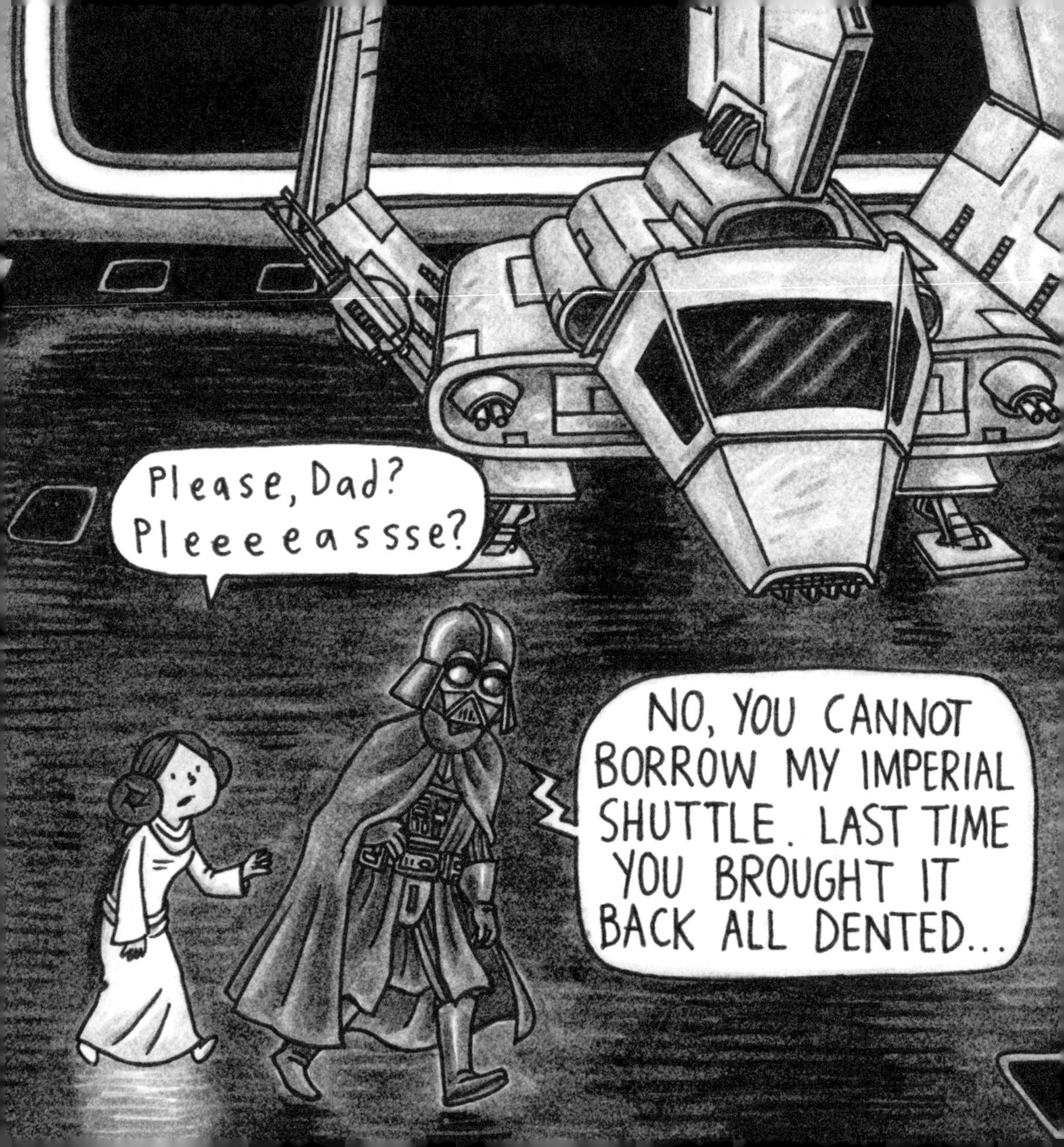
Please, Dad? Pleeeeeassse?
NO, YOU CANNOT BORROW MY IMPERIAL SHUTTLE. LAST TIME YOU BROUGHT IT BACK ALL DENTED...

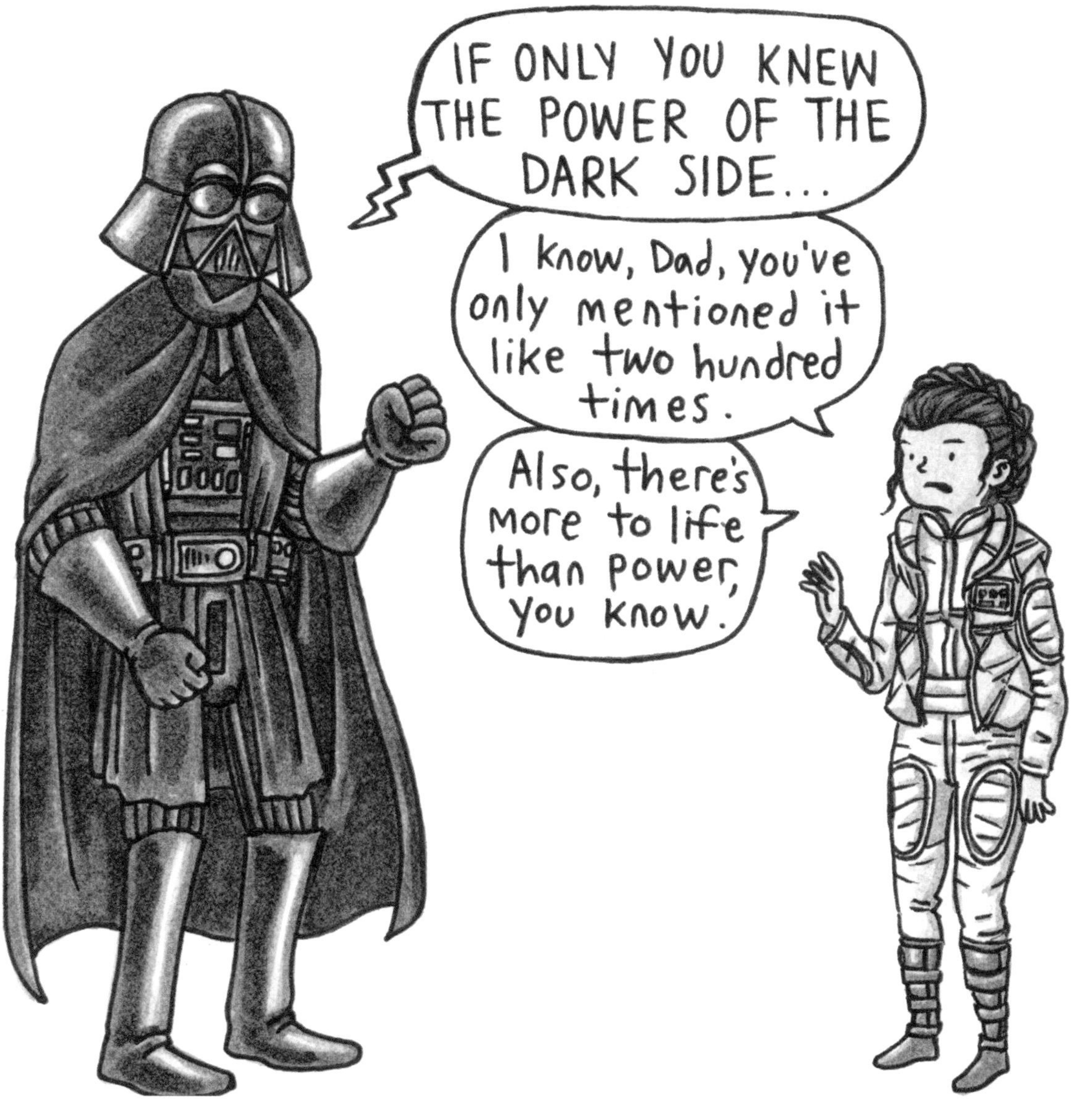
IF ONLY YOU KNEW THE POWER OF THE DARK SIDE...
I know, Dad, you've only mentioned it like two hundred times.
Also, there's more to life than power, you know.

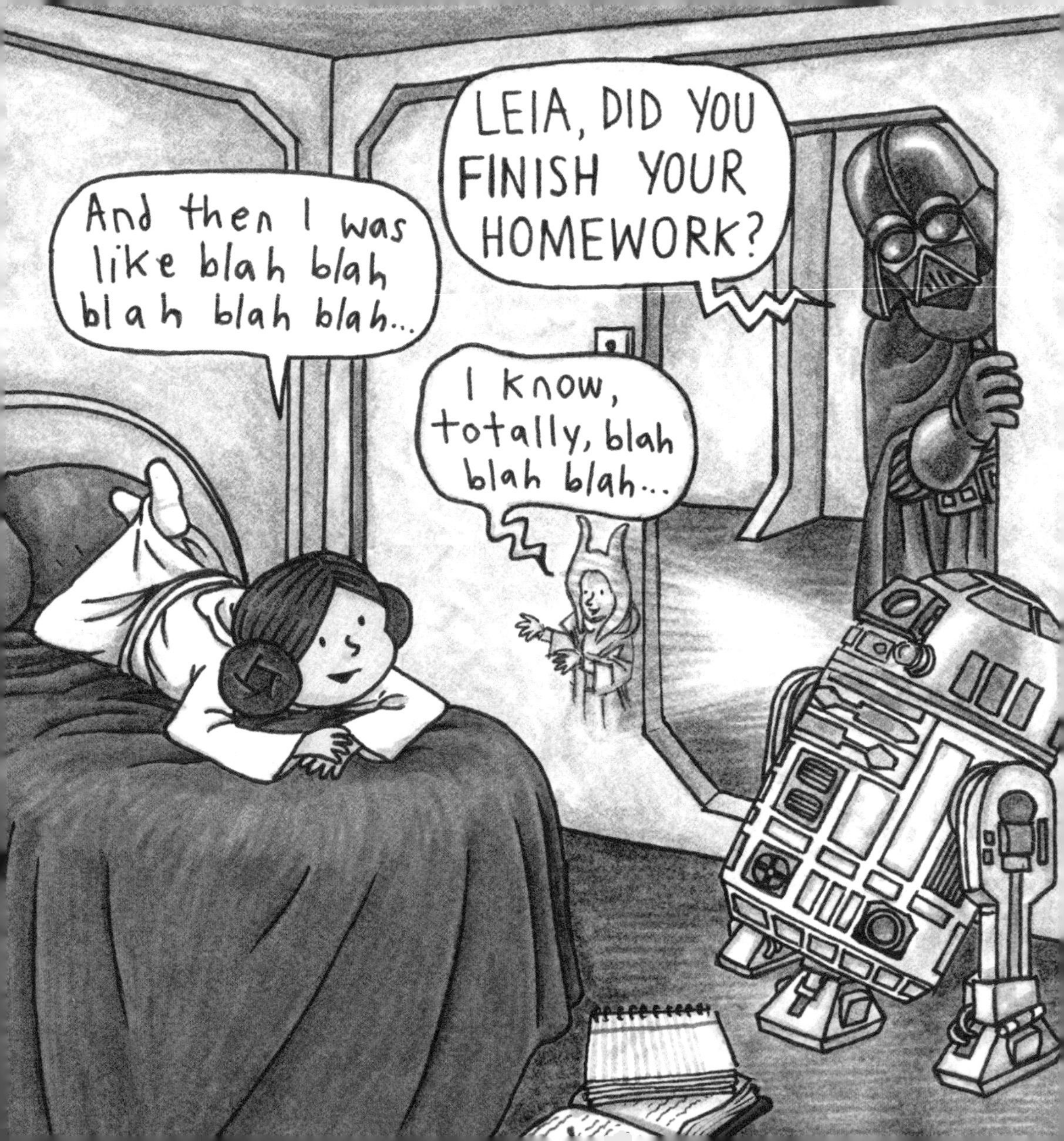
And then I was like blah blah blah blah blah...
LEIA, DID YOU FINISH YOUR HOMEWORK?
I know, totally, blah blah blah...

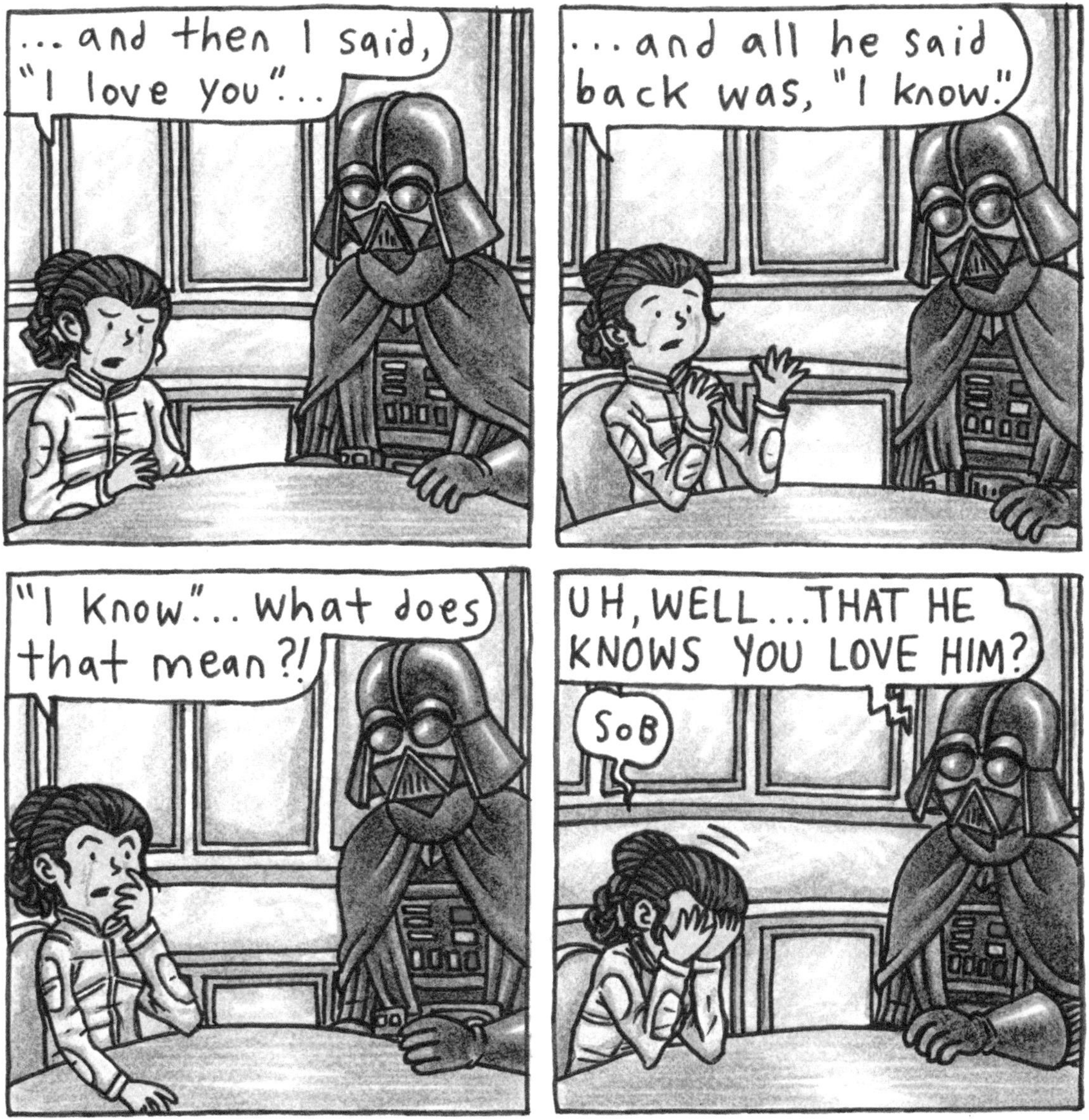
...and then I said, "I love you"...
...and all he said back was, "I know."
"I know"... What does that mean?!
UH, WELL...THAT HE KNOWS YOU LOVE HIM?
SoB

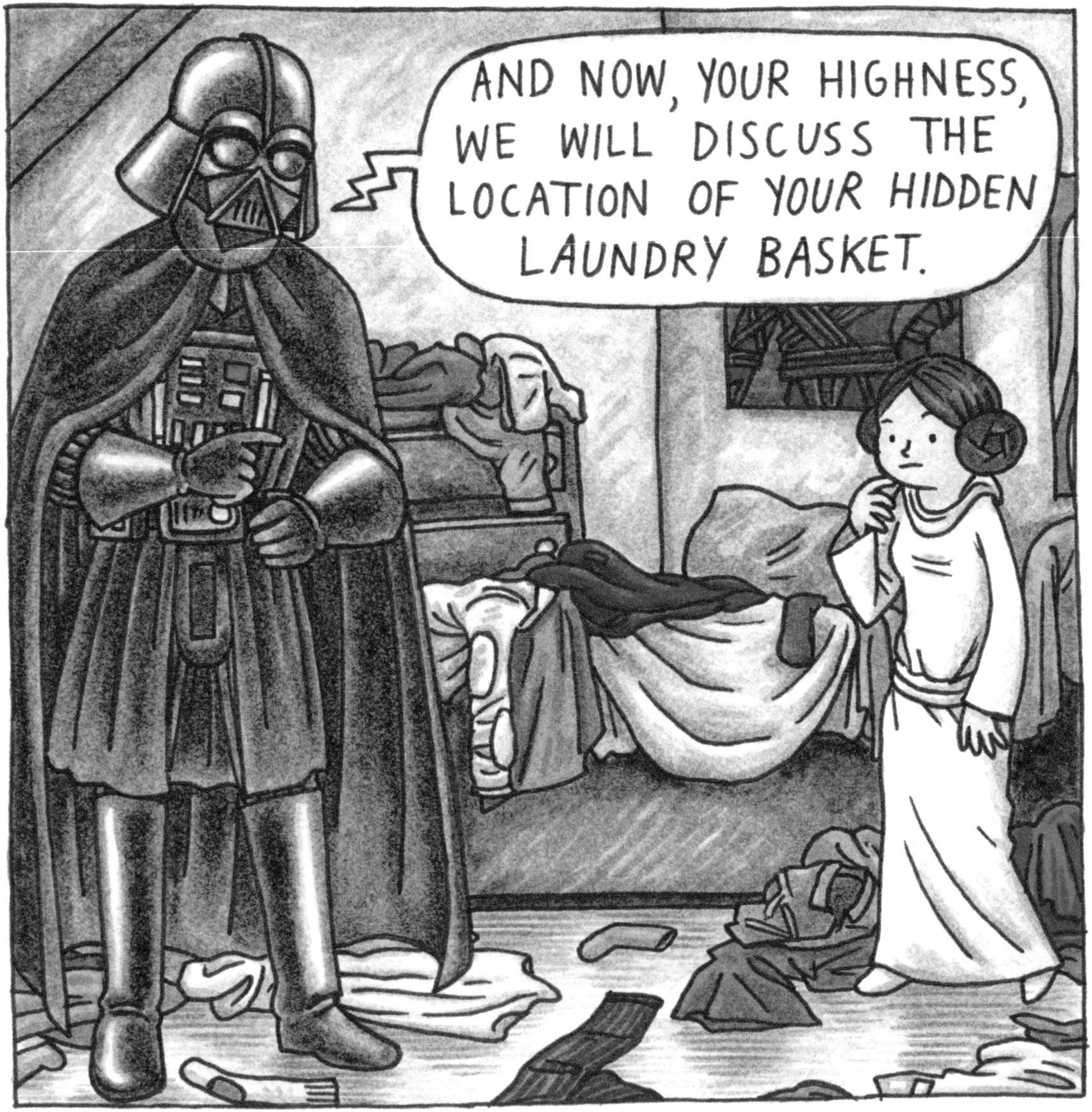
AND NOW, YOUR HIGHNESS, WE WILL DISCUSS THE LOCATION OF YOUR HIDDEN LAUNDRY BASKET.

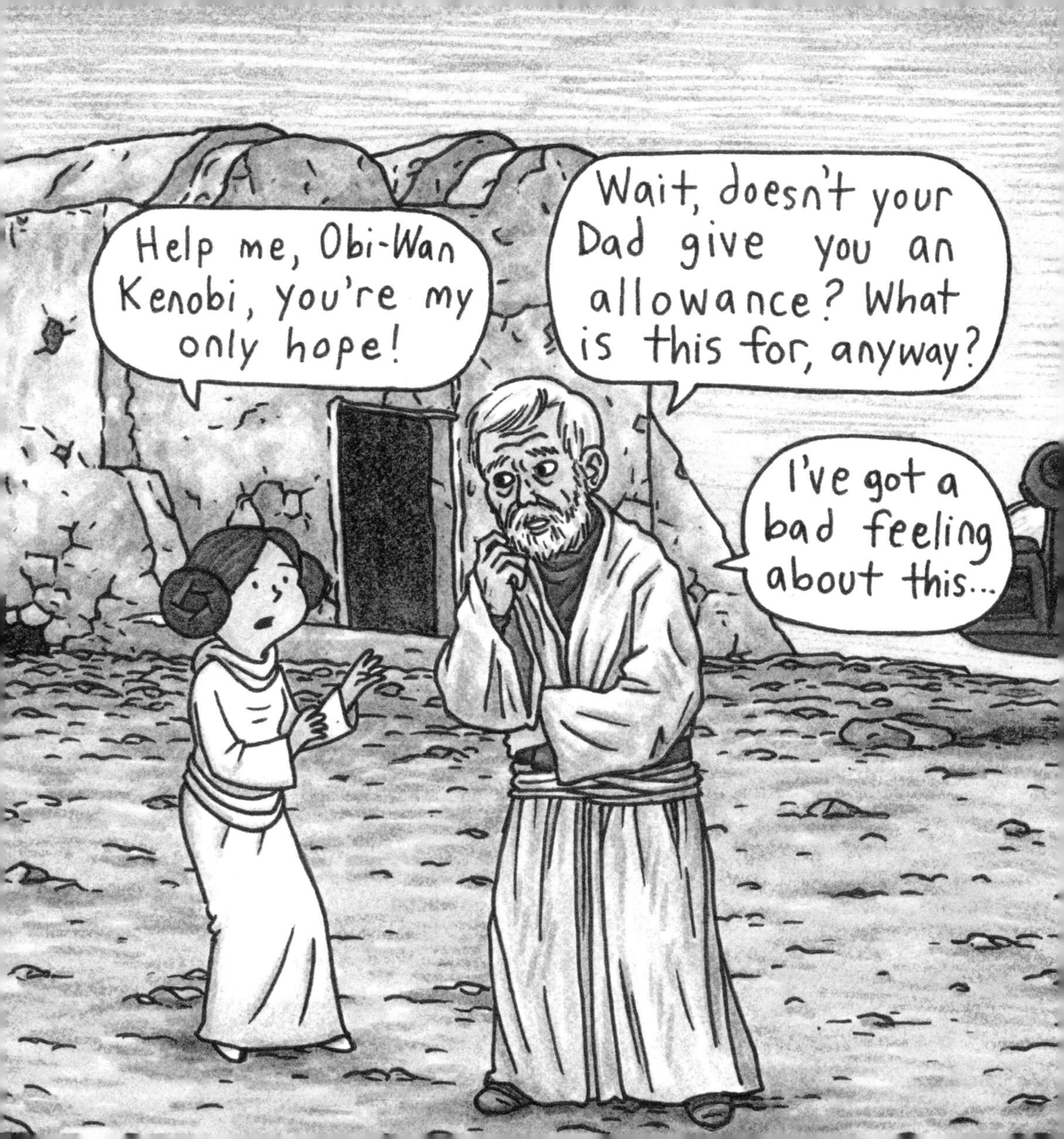
Help me, Obi-Wan Kenobi, you're my only hope!
Wait, doesn't your Dad give you an allowance? What is this for, anyway?
I've got a bad feeling about this...

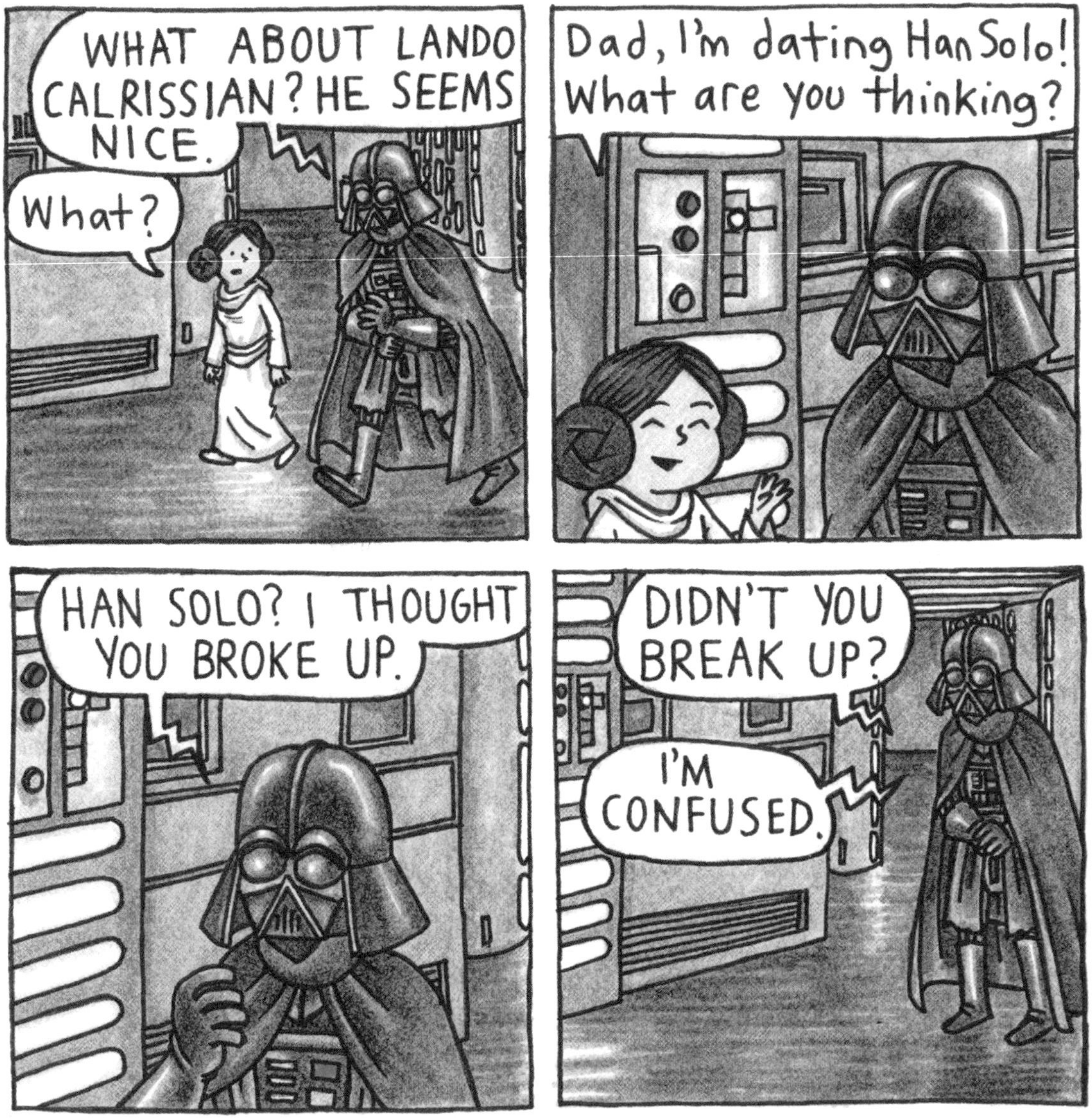
WHAT ABOUT LANDO CALRISSIAN? HE SEEMS NICE.
What?
Dad, I'm dating Han Solo! What are you thinking?
HAN SOLO? I THOUGHT YOU BROKE UP.
DIDN'T YOU BREAK UP?
I'M CONFUSED.

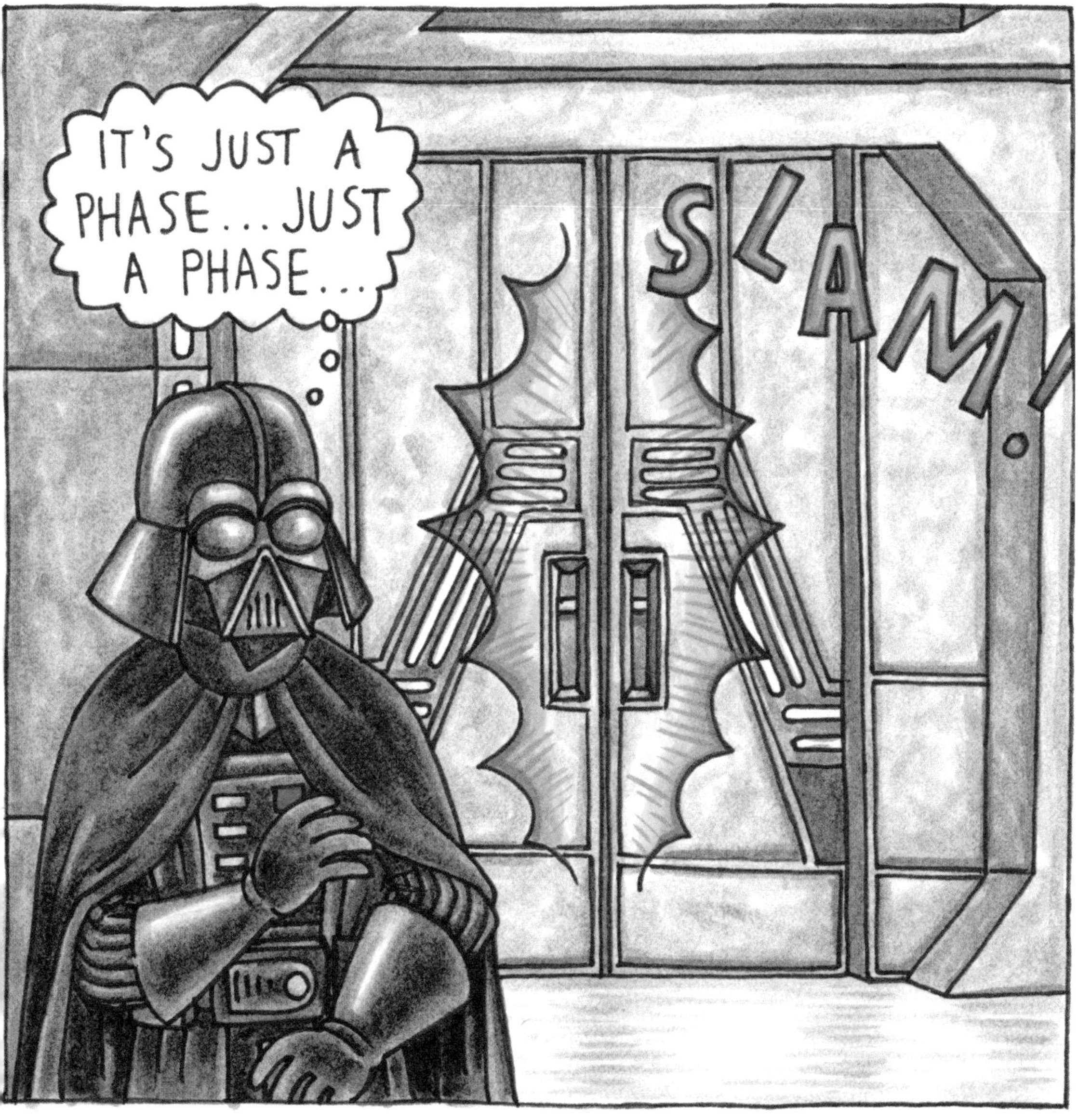
IT'S JUST A PHASE... JUST A PHASE...
SLAM!

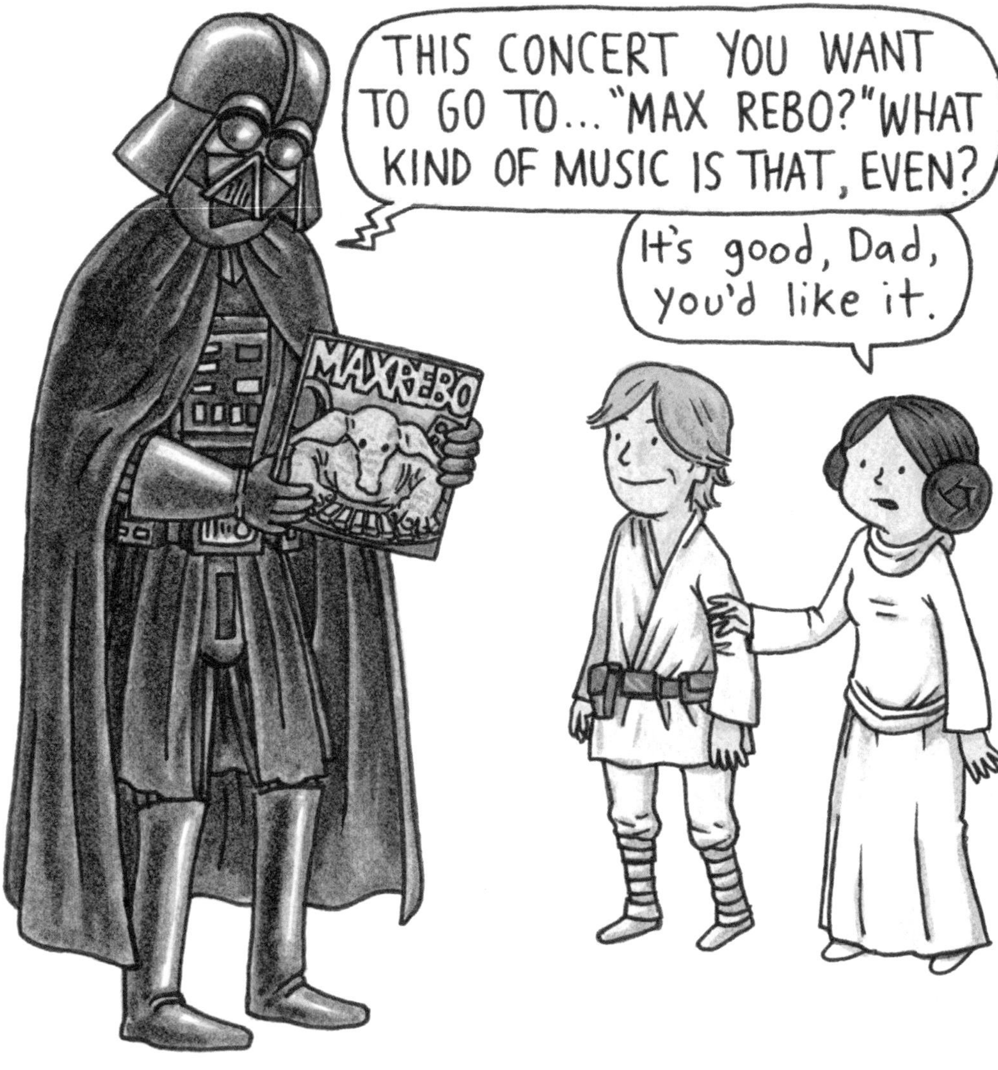
THIS CONCERT YOU WANT TO GO TO... "MAX REBO?" WHAT KIND OF MUSIC IS THAT, EVEN?
It's good, Dad, you'd like it.
MAX REBO

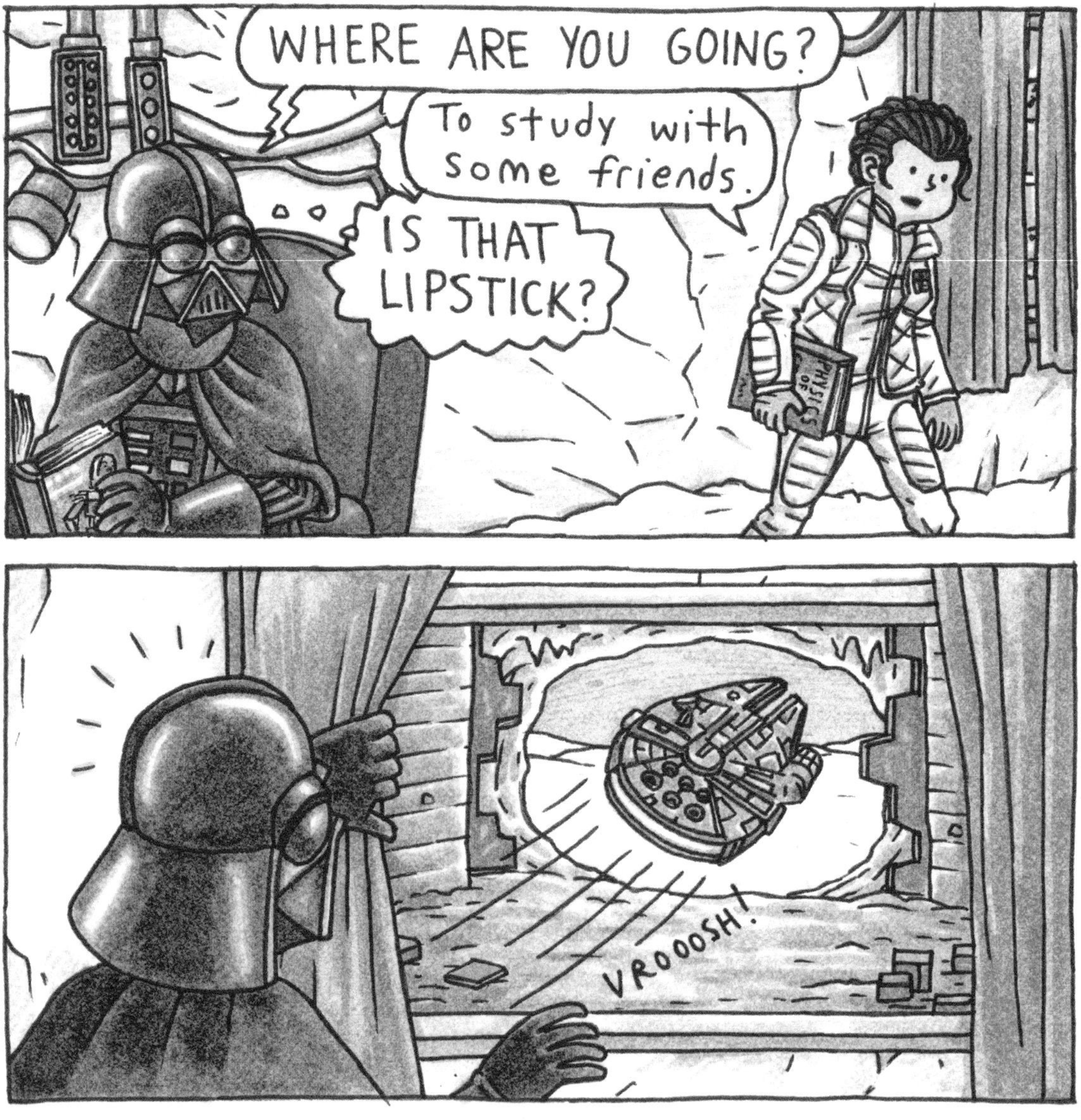
WHERE ARE YOU GOING?
To study with some friends.
IS THAT LIPSTICK?
VROOOSH!

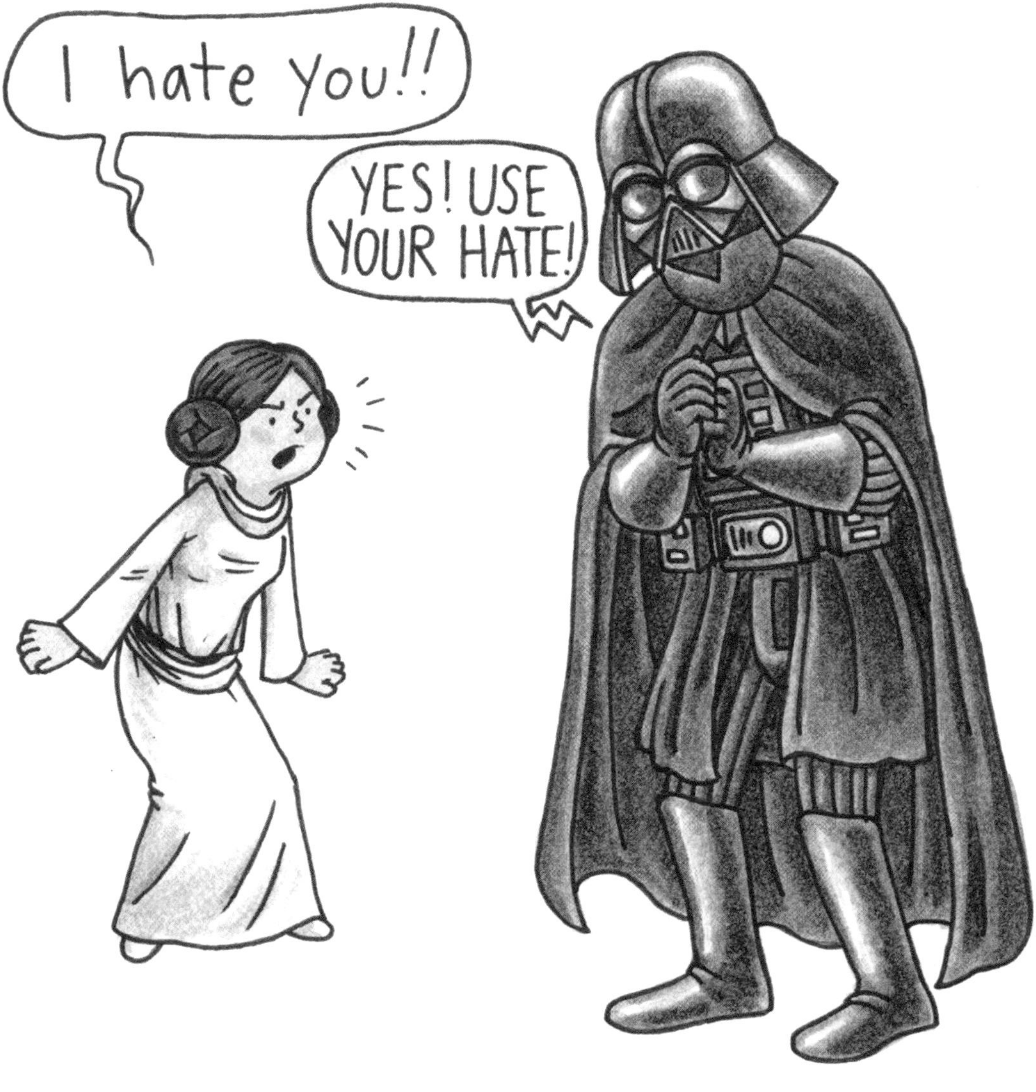
I hate you!!
YES! USE YOUR HATE!

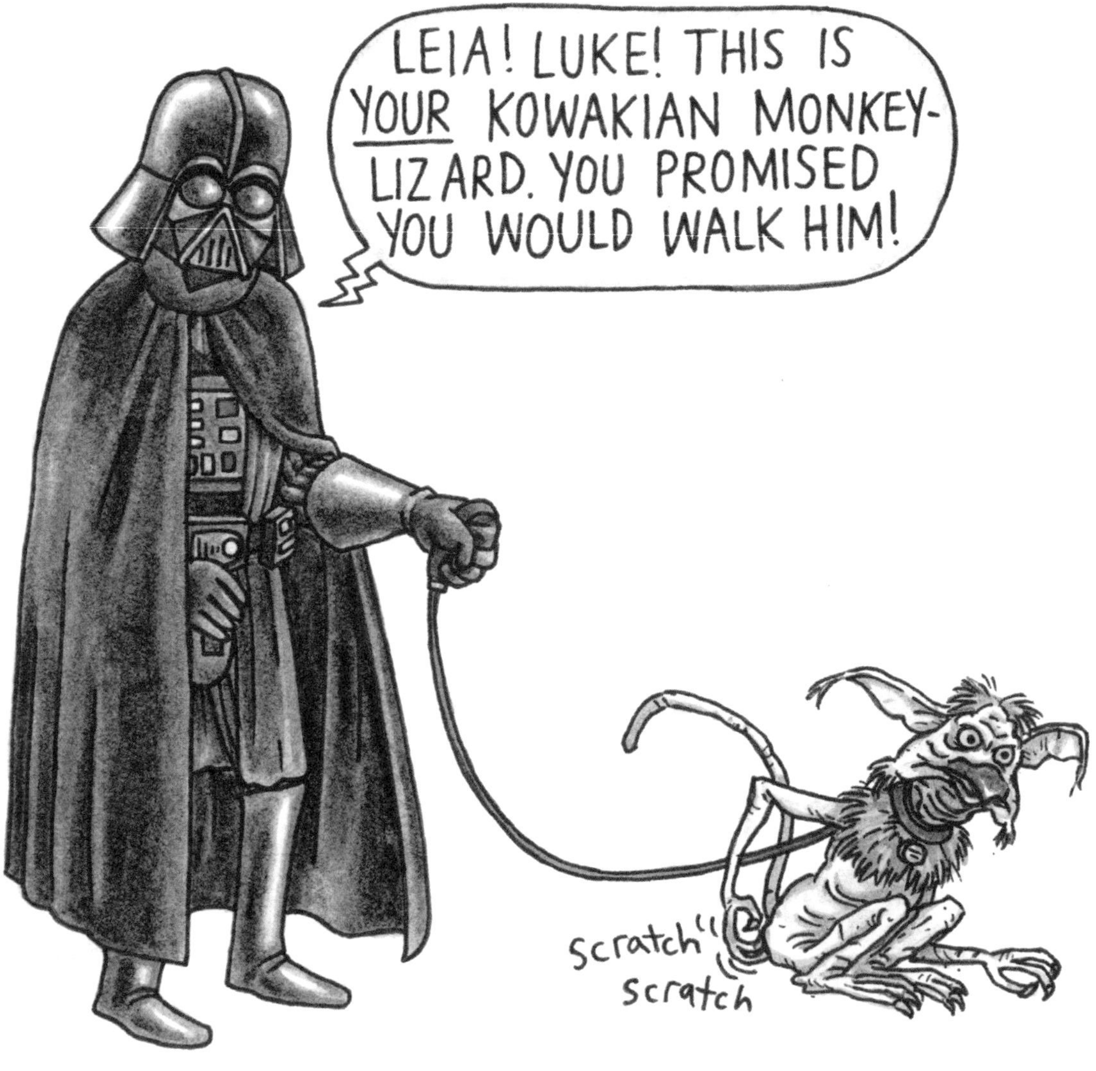
LEIA! LUKE! THIS IS YOUR KOWAKIAN MONKEY-LIZARD. YOU PROMISED YOU WOULD WALK HIM!
scratch
scratch

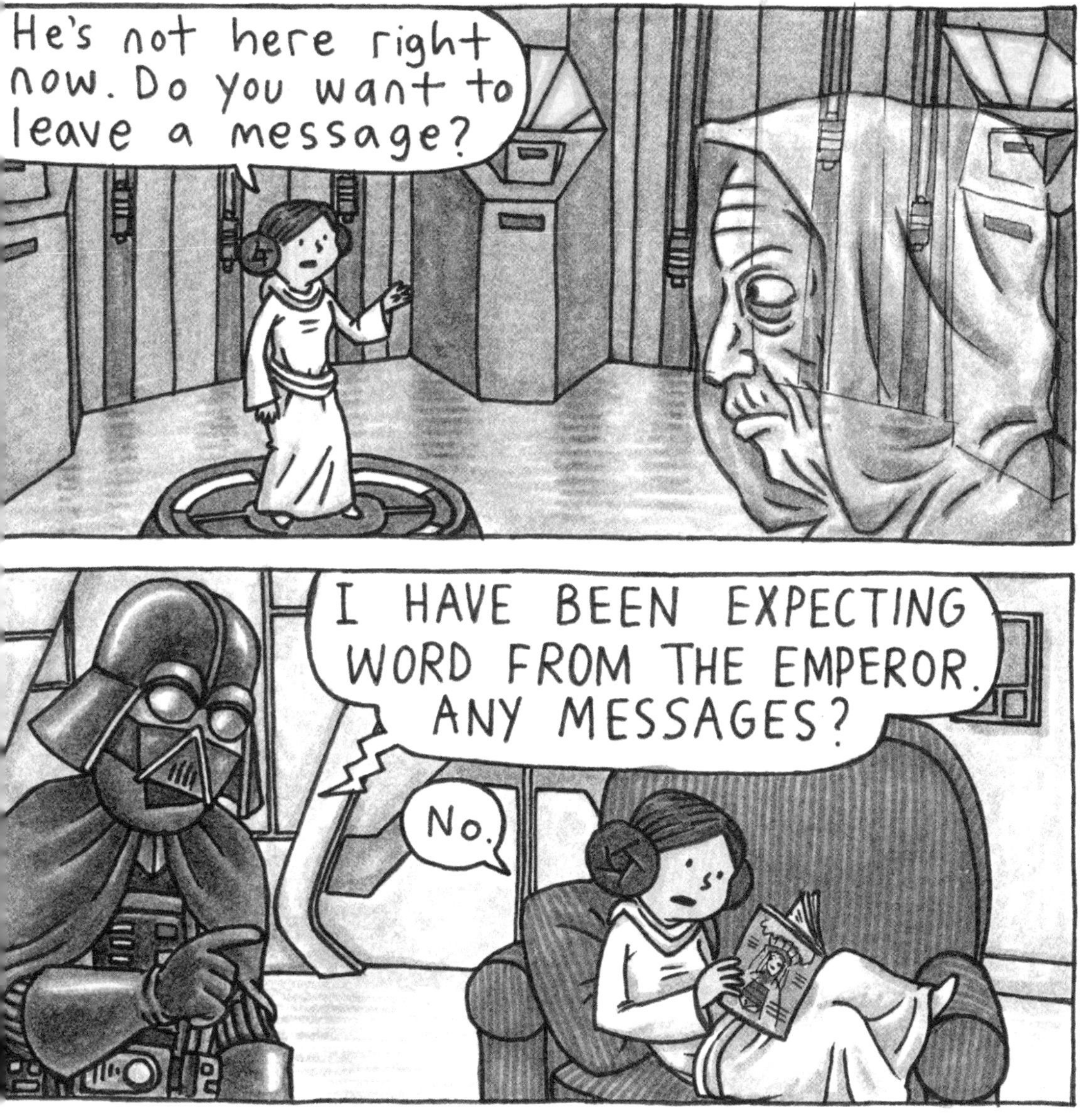
He's not here right now. Do you want to leave a message?
I HAVE BEEN EXPECTING WORD FROM THE EMPEROR. ANY MESSAGES?
No.

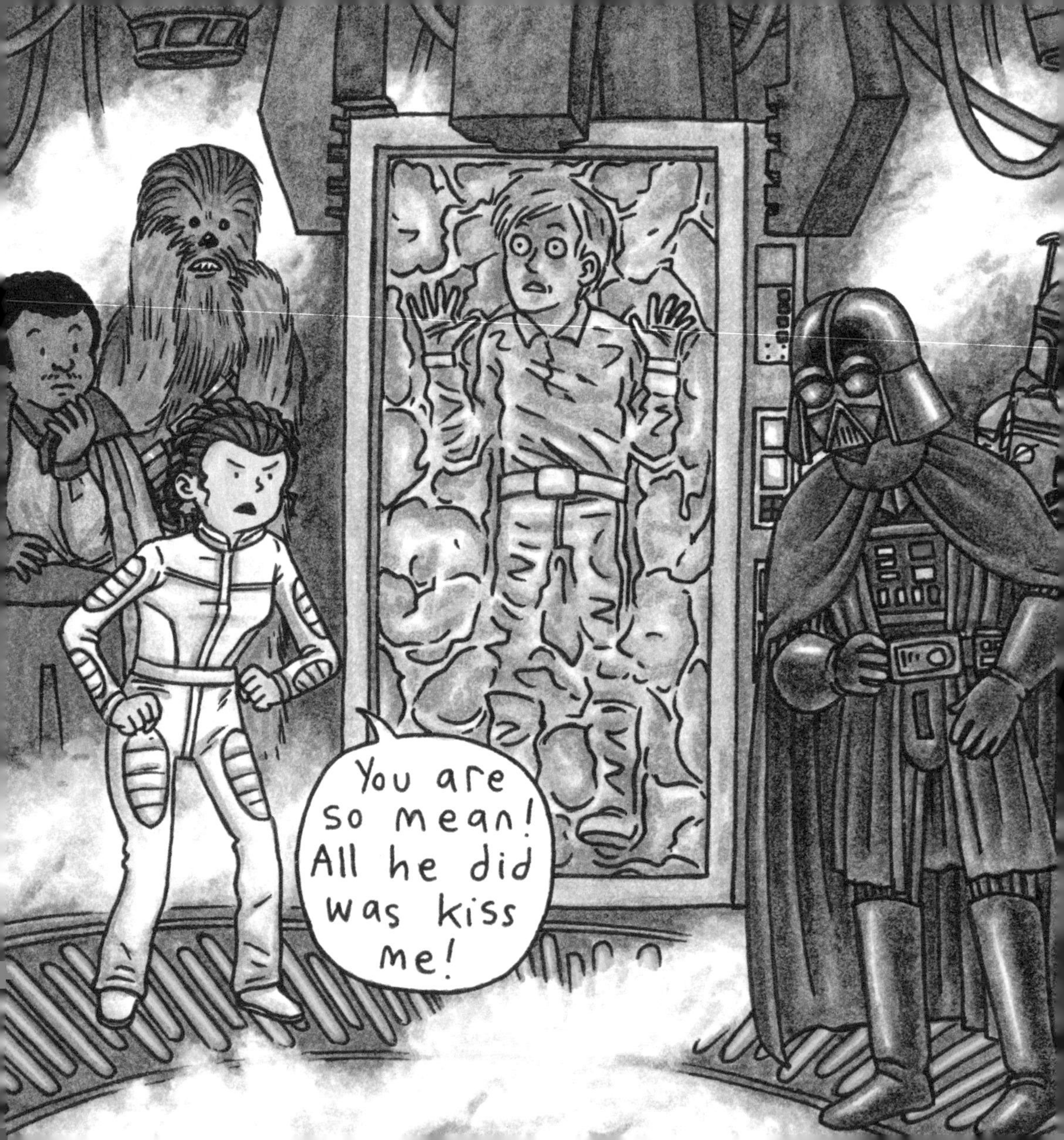
You are so mean! All he did was kiss me!

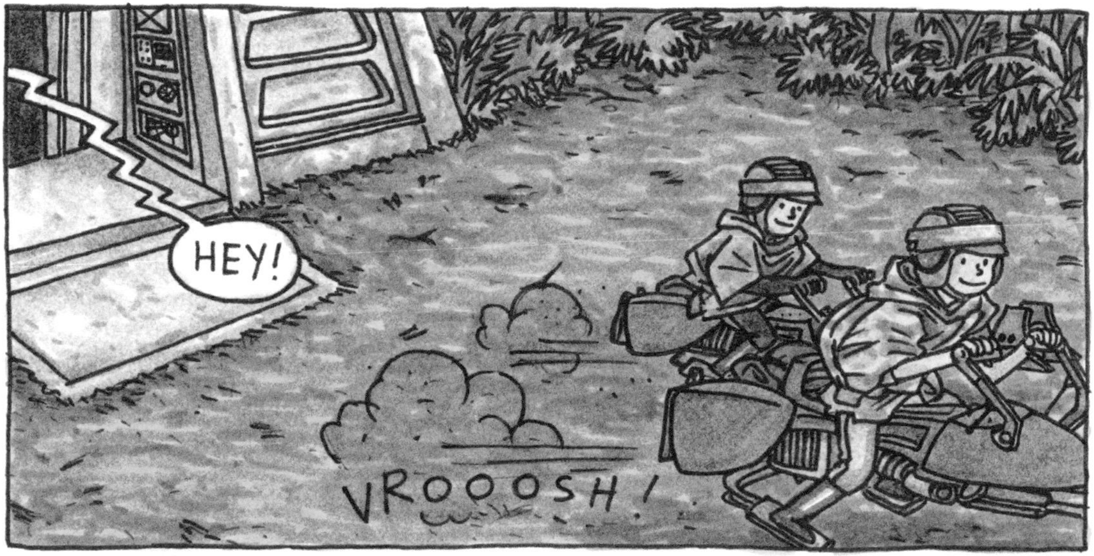
HEY!
VROOOSH!

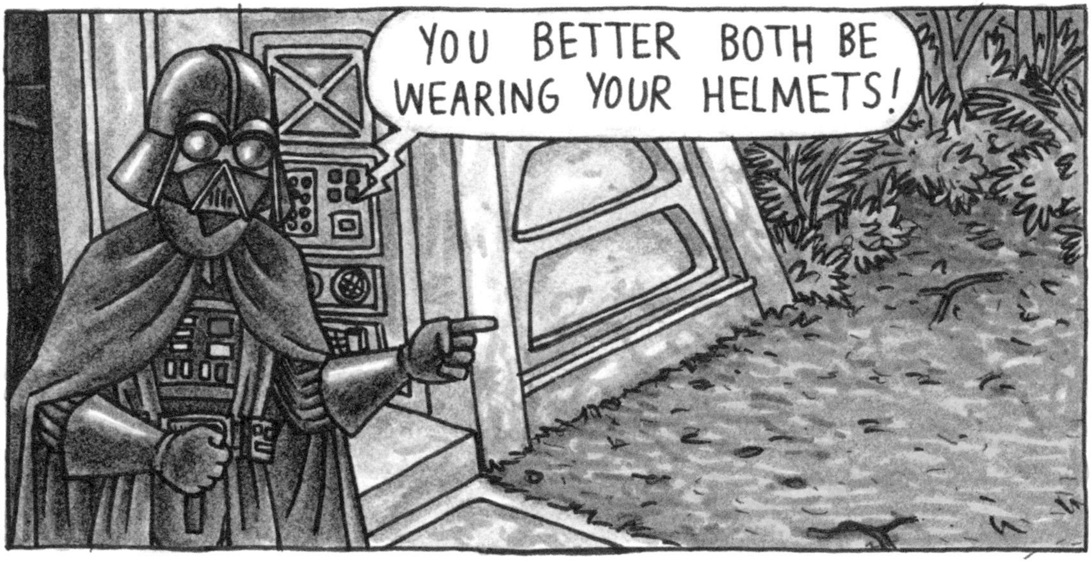
YOU BETTER BOTH BE WEARING YOUR HELMETS!

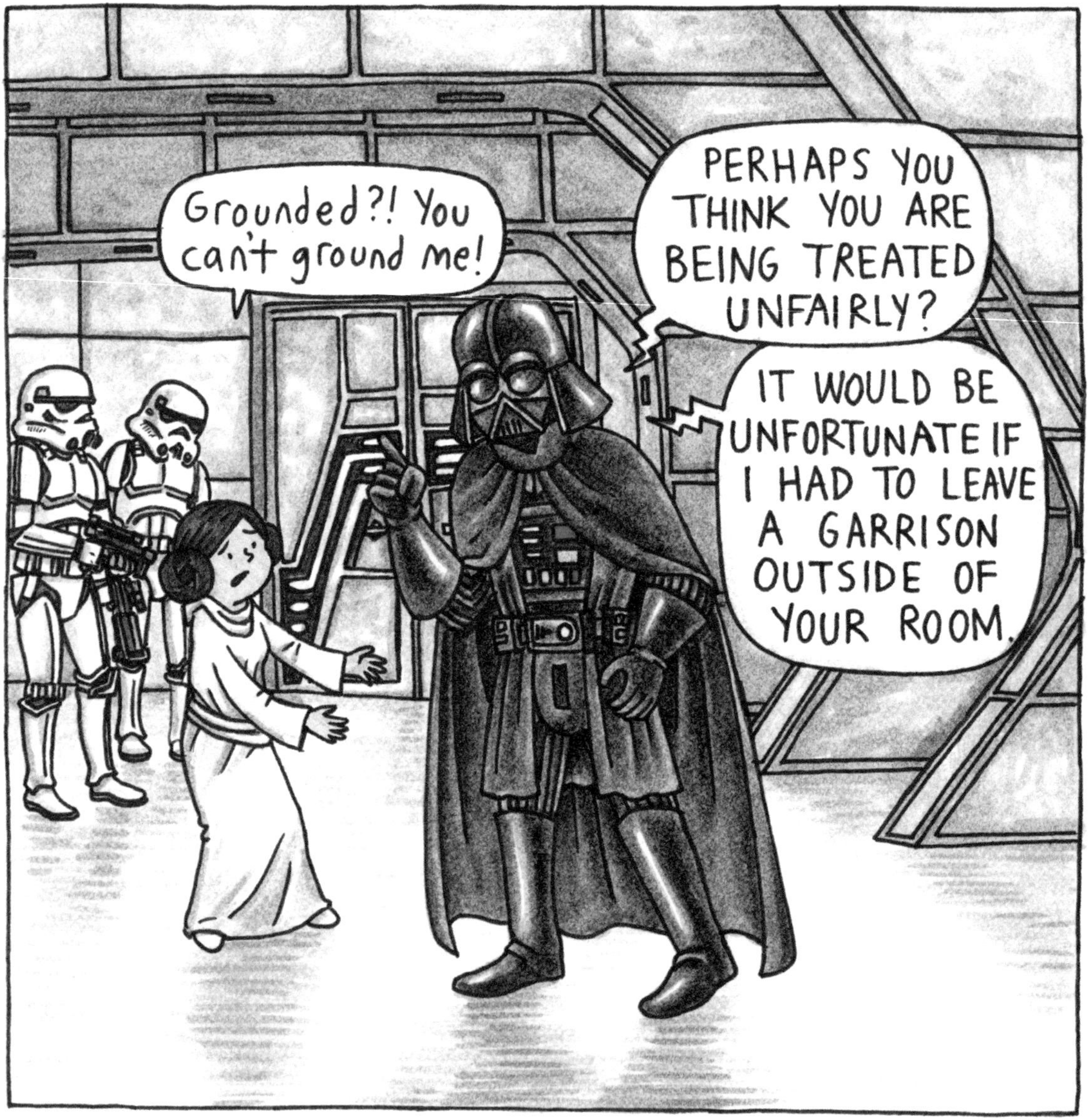
Grounded?! You can't ground me!
PERHAPS YOU THINK YOU ARE BEING TREATED UNFAIRLY?
IT WOULD BE UNFORTUNATE IF I HAD TO LEAVE A GARRISON OUTSIDE OF YOUR ROOM.

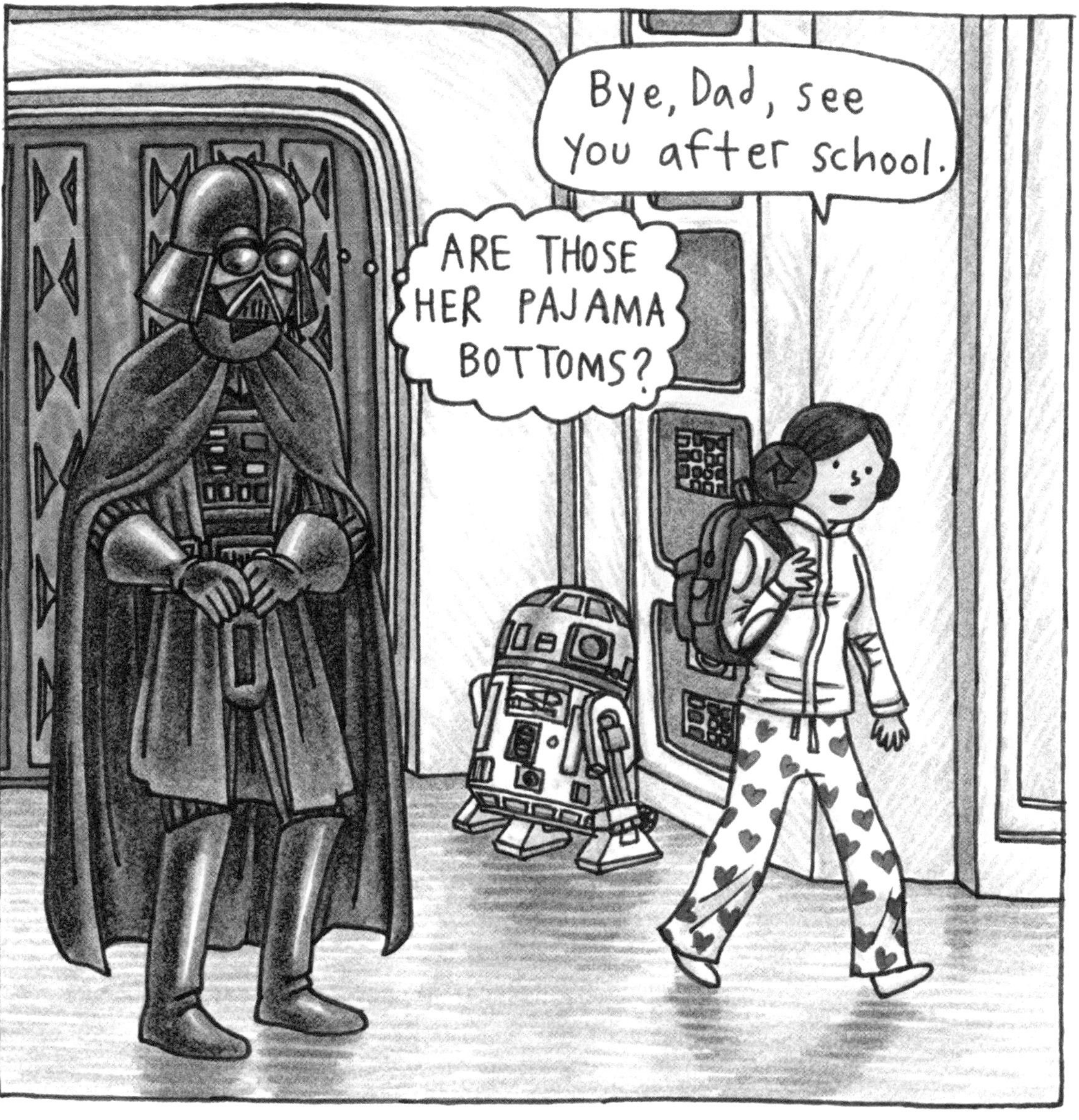
Bye, Dad, see you after school.
ARE THOSE HER PAJAMA BOTTOMS?

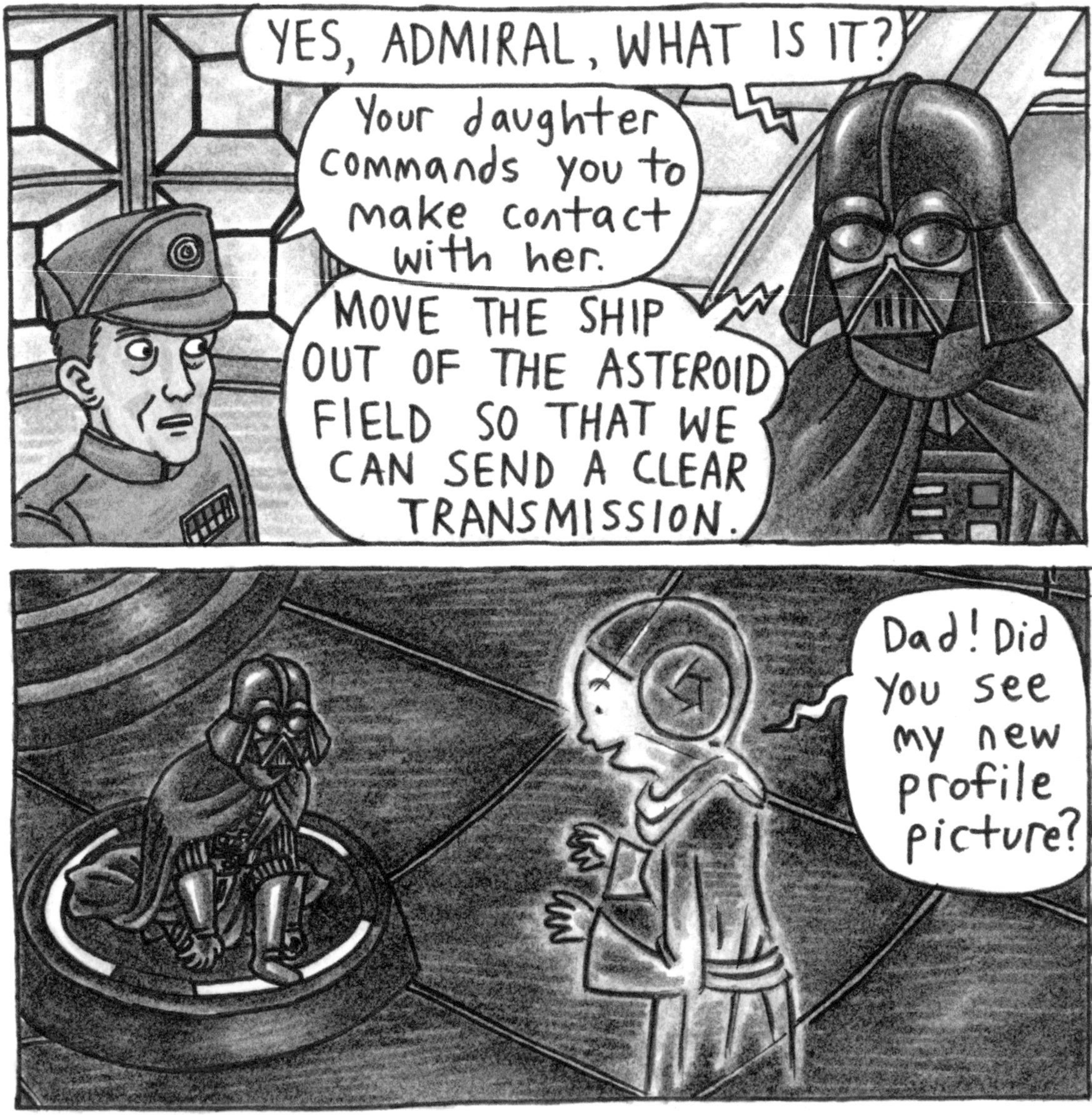
YES, ADMIRAL, WHAT IS IT?
Your daughter commands you to make contact with her.
MOVE THE SHIP OUT OF THE ASTEROID FIELD SO THAT WE CAN SEND A CLEAR TRANSMISSION.
Dad! Did you see my new profile picture?

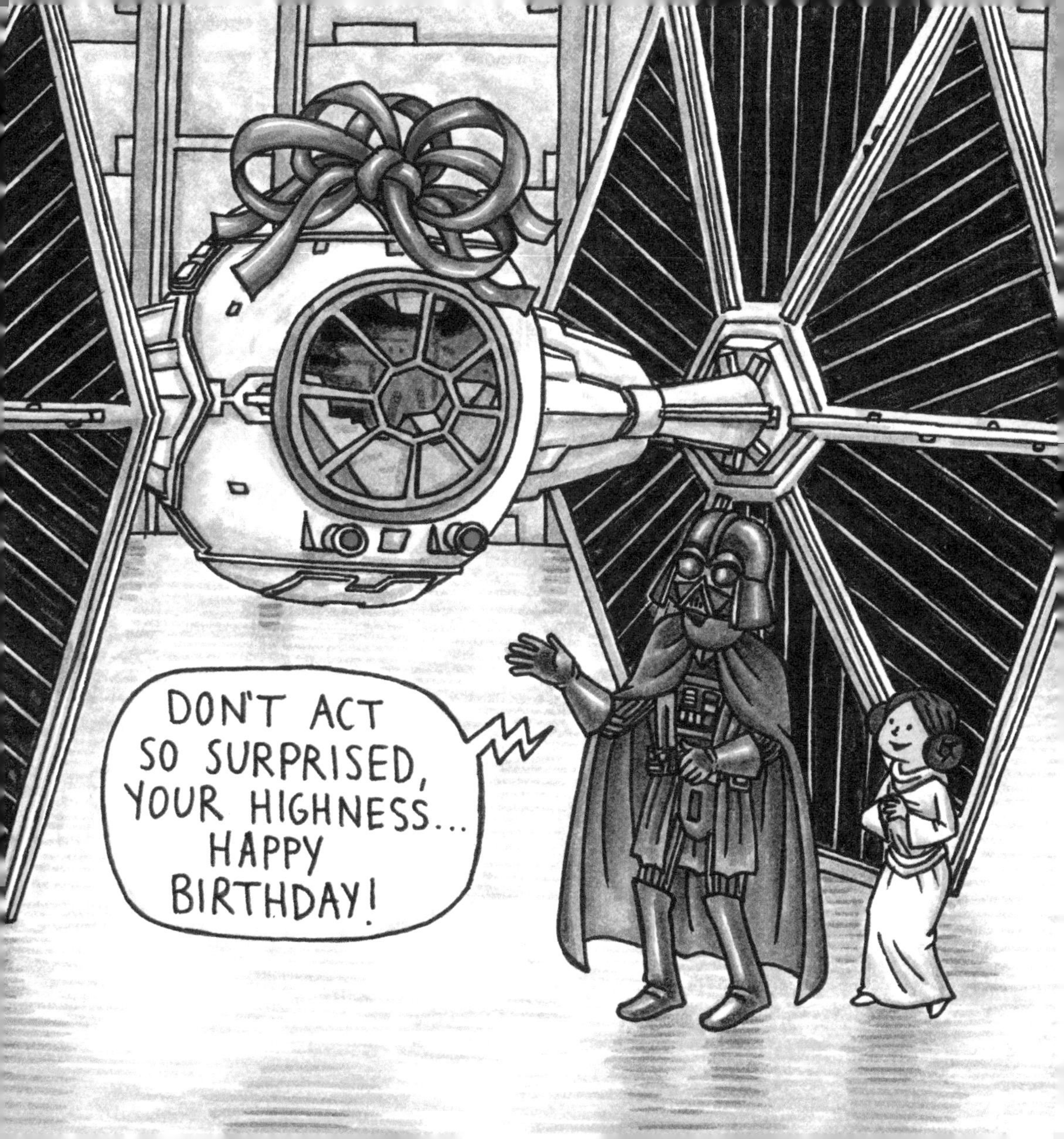
DON'T ACT SO SURPRISED, YOUR HIGHNESS... HAPPY BIRTHDAY!

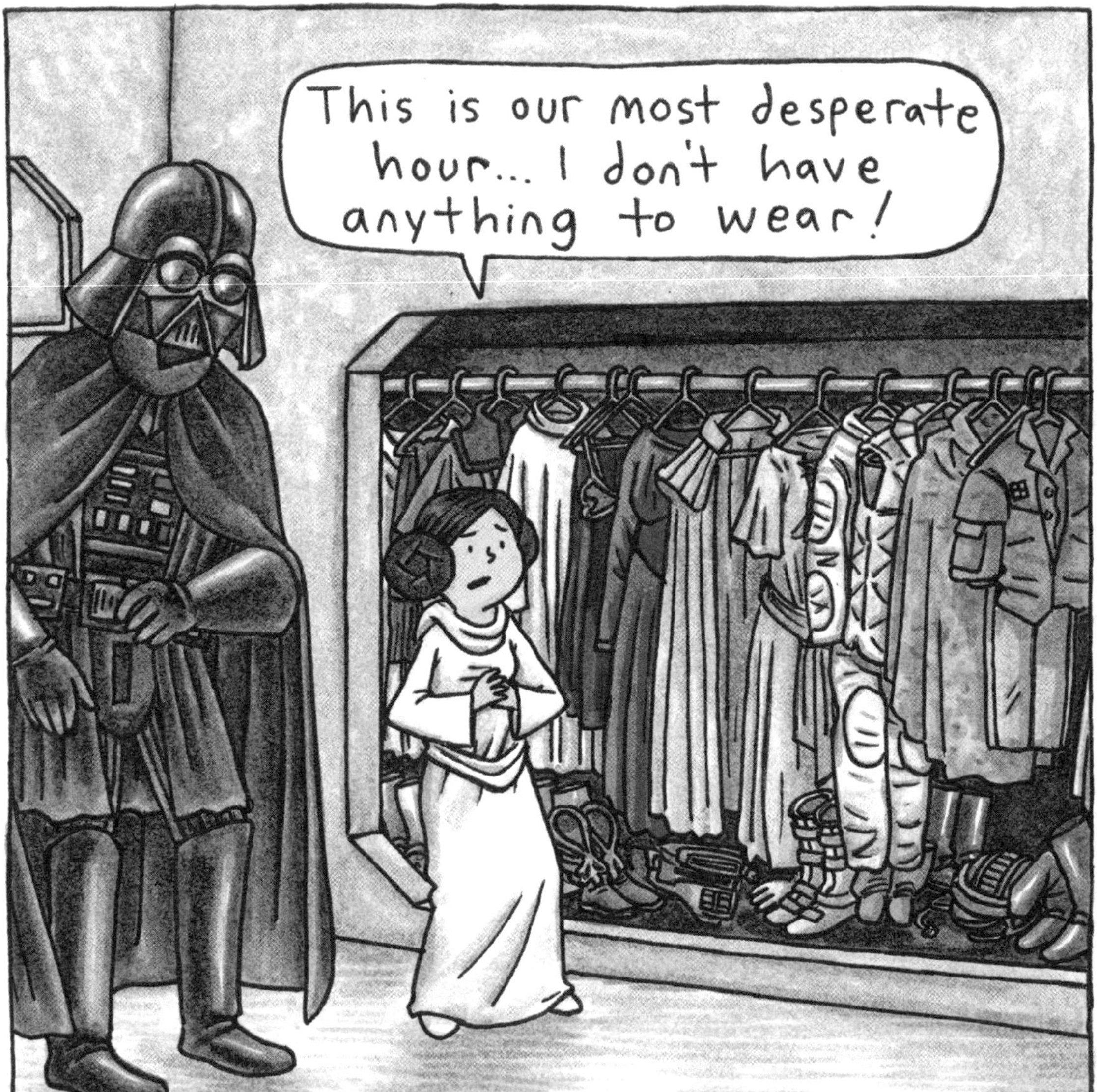
This is our most desperate hour... I don't have anything to wear!

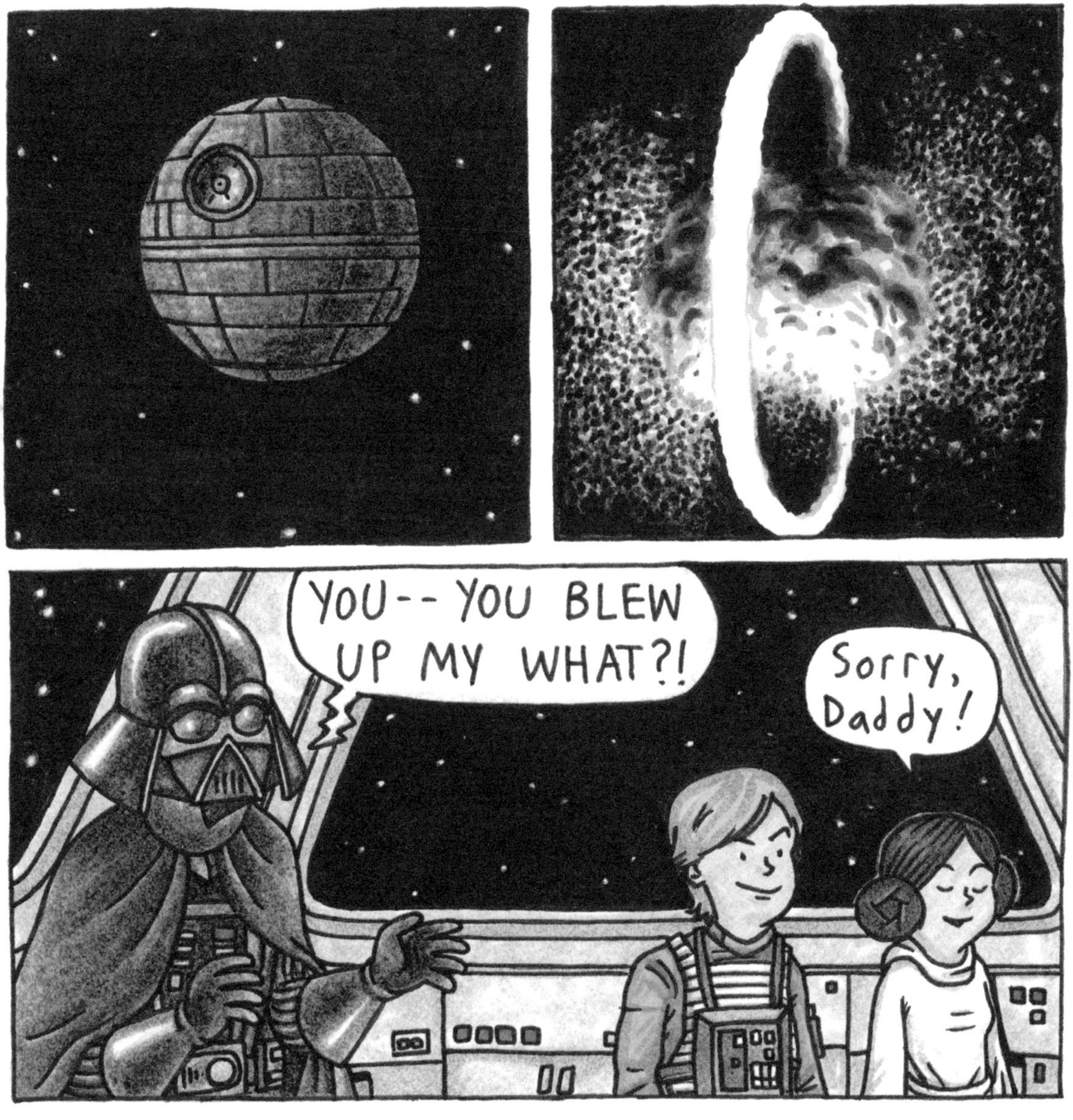
YOU-- YOU BLEW UP MY WHAT?!
Sorry, Daddy!

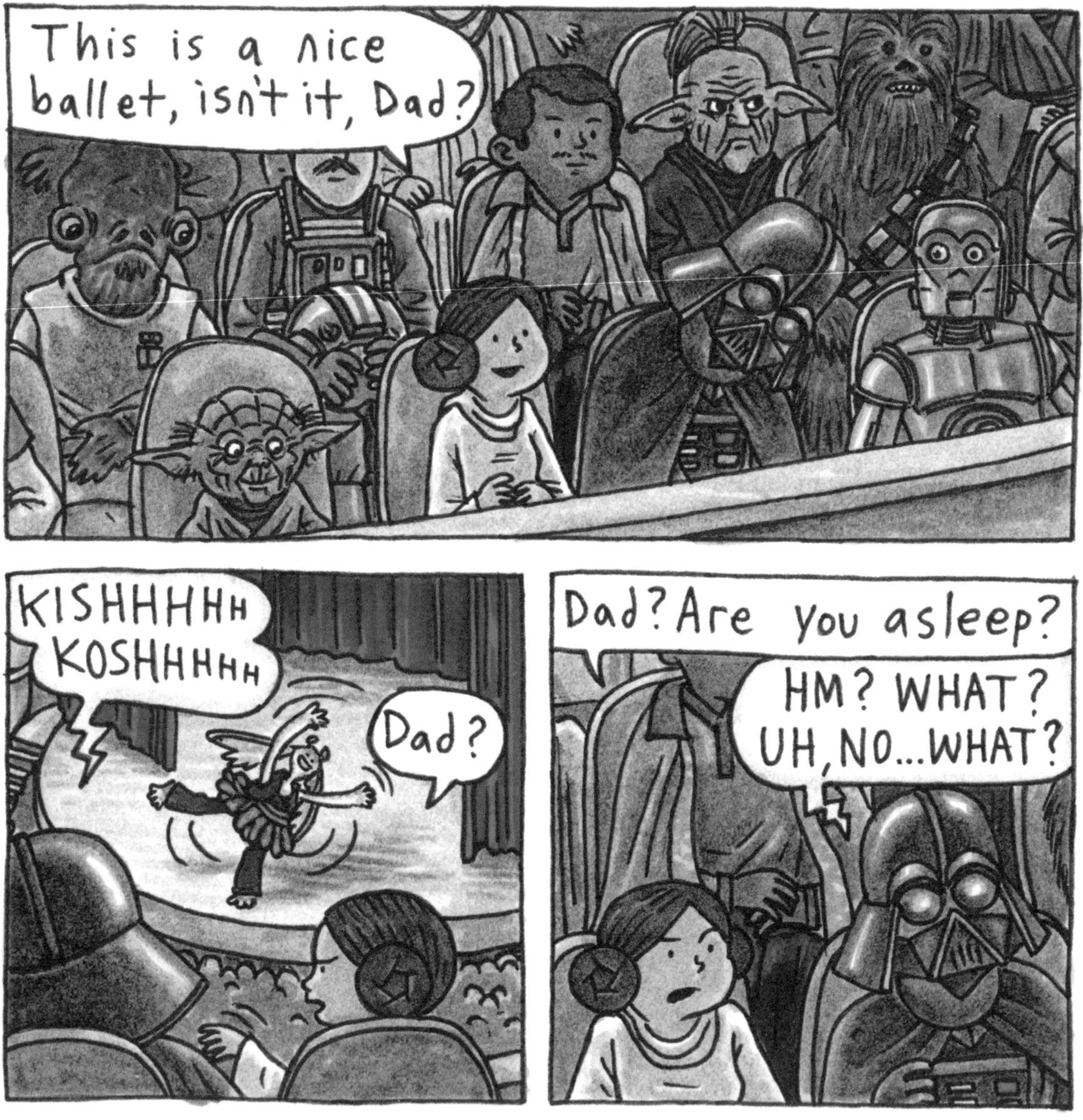
This is a nice ballet, isn't it, Dad?
KISHHHHH KOSHHHHH
Dad?
Dad? Are you asleep?
HM? WHAT? UH, NO...WHAT?

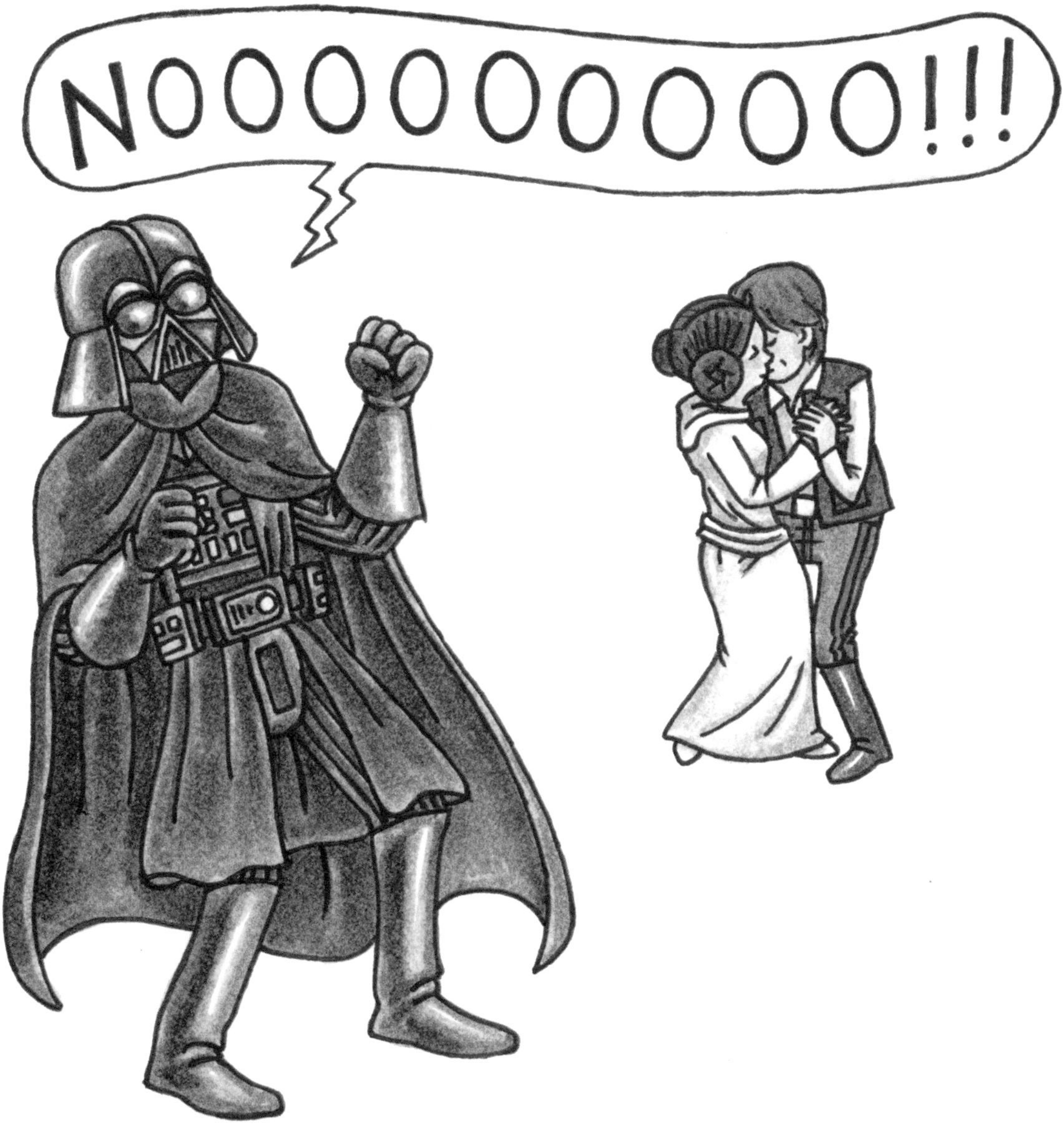
NOOOOOOOOOO!!!

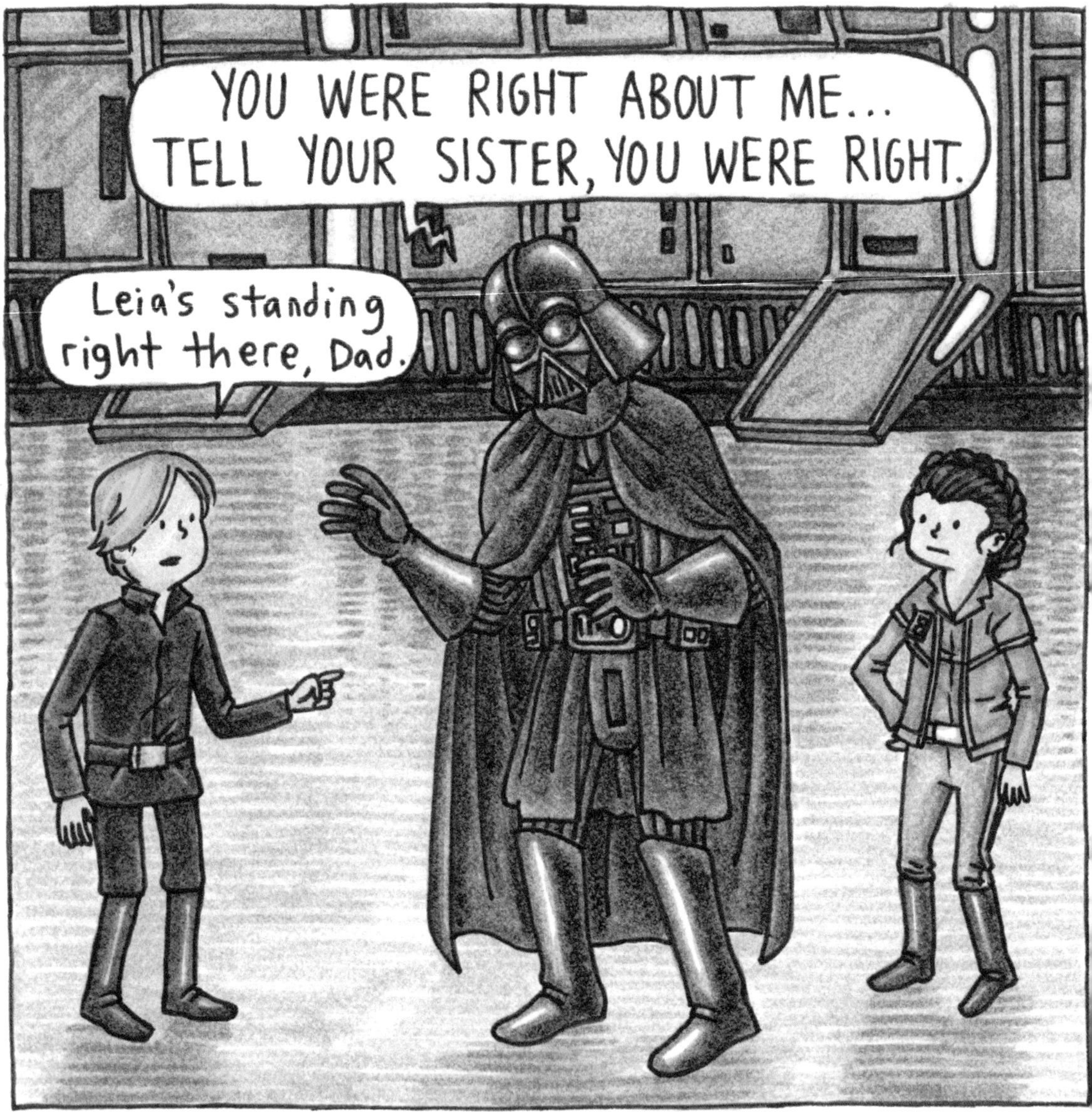
YOU WERE RIGHT ABOUT ME... TELL YOUR SISTER, YOU WERE RIGHT.
Leia's standing right there, Dad.

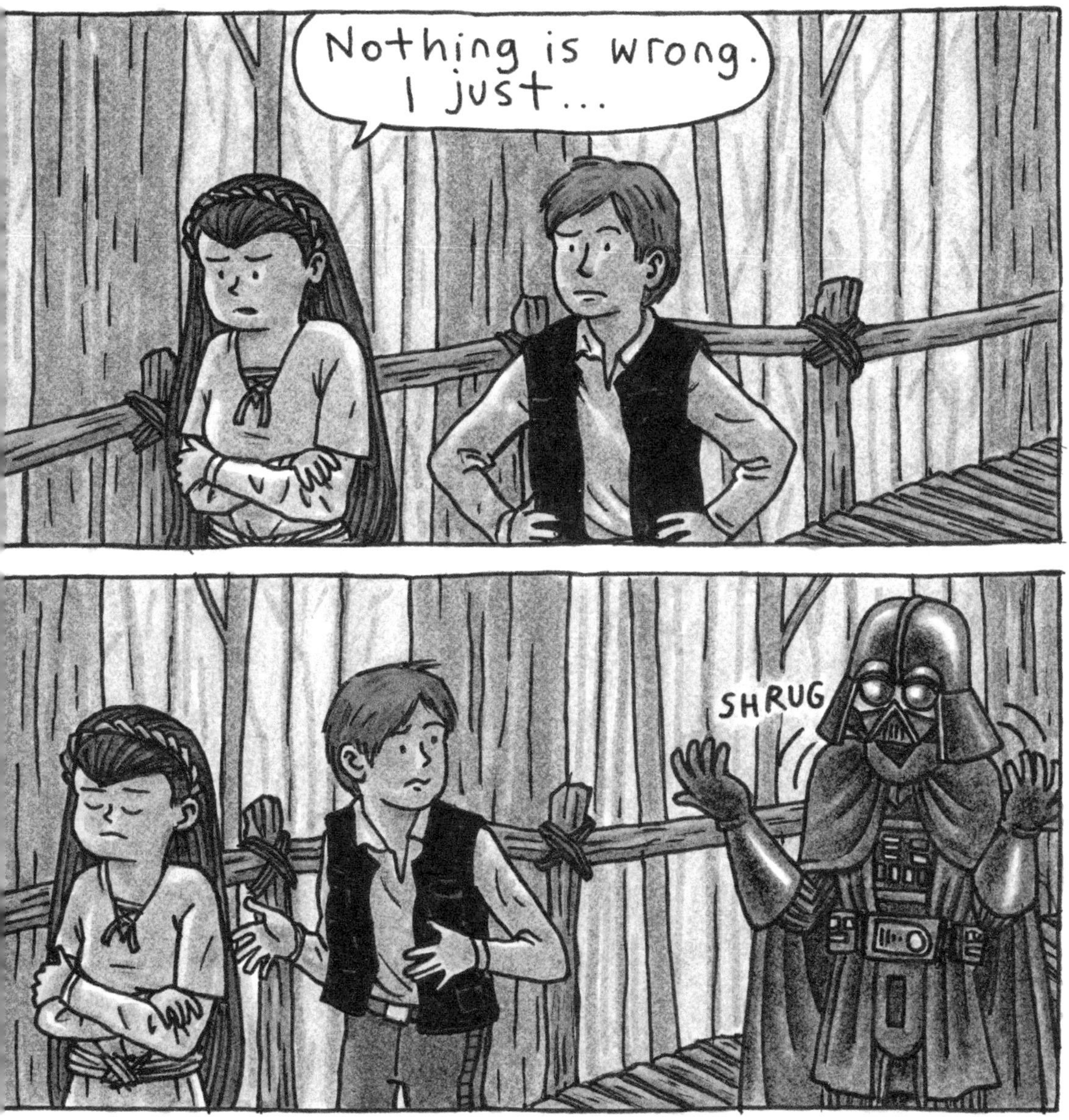
Nothing is wrong. I just...
SHRUG

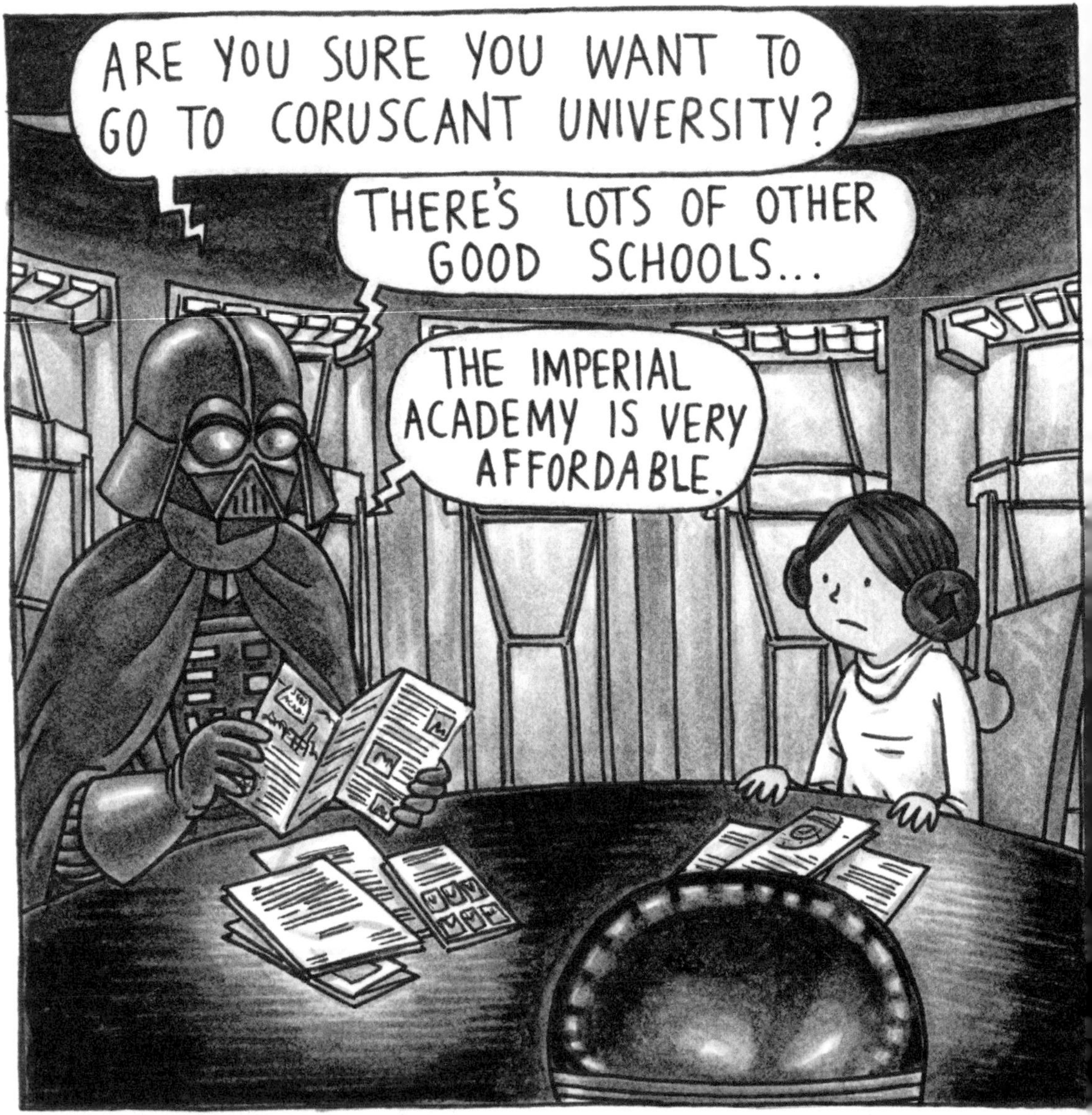
ARE YOU SURE YOU WANT TO GO TO CORUSCANT UNIVERSITY?
THERE'S LOTS OF OTHER GOOD SCHOOLS...
THE IMPERIAL ACADEMY IS VERY AFFORDABLE.

~BLUSH

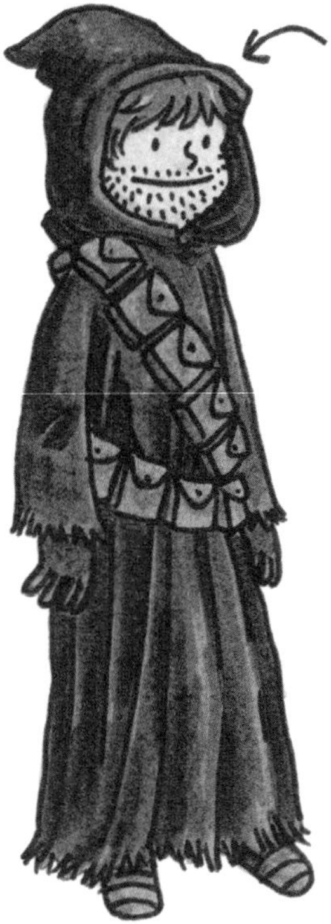

Jeffrey Brown is best known for his autobiographical comics and humorous graphic novels. He grew up watching Star Wars, playing with Star Wars action figures, and collecting Star Wars trading cards. He lives in Chicago with his wife and two sons.

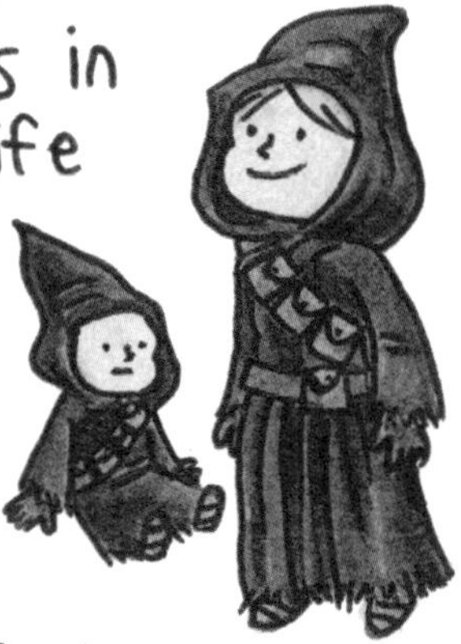

P.O. Box 120
DEERFIELD IL
60015-0120
USA

WWW.JEFFREYBROWNCOMICS.COM

MORE BOOKS BY JEFFREY BROWN

From Chronicle (WWW.CHRONICLEBOOKS.COM)

Cat Getting Out Of A Bag
Cats Are Weird
Darth Vader and Son